HISTORIC HAUNTS
FLORIDA

JAMIE ROUSH

Inquiries should be addressed to:

Jamie Roush
historichaunts@yahoo.com

Foreward:

In this book I tried to include any and all personal experiences I had at each of the locations I've written about. Unfortunately, ghosts, as I like to say, do not perform on cue. In situations where my personal experiences were limited, I tried to interview people who lived or worked at the locations, past or present. Hours of research, traveling to the different locations, visiting, investigating, touring, and interviewing, all went into writing this book and I loved every moment of it! I have heard a lot of fascinating stories, experienced a lot of paranormal activity, and have made new friends. I look forward to starting on the next volume of Historic Haunts.

Dedication:

First of all, I want to thank my mom, Gayel Roush, for all her support and love. You have always been there for me and I couldn't have made it without an awesome mom like you! Thanks, mom! I love ya!!
~Munchkin

I also want to thank the love of my life, Deric Pearce, for all your help and support on getting this book finally finished! You are the most amazing person I have ever met. I love you with all my heart!
XOX,
~Jamie

Special Thanks:

Assistant Investigator: Gayel Roush

Editing: Deric Pearce & Paula Dillon

Design and Layout: Deric Pearce
All Photographs are credited to their photographers
Additional photography provided by and copyright Big Stock

Third Printing Sept 2013
ISBN: 978-0-578-09644-5

HISTORIC HAUNTS FLORIDA

Table of Contents

A GHOST OF THE CONFEDERACY
Fort Barrancas, Pensacola, FL

An Inspiring Fort

As I was making my way to St. Francisville, Louisiana for an investigation, I had some spare time on my hands and decided to stop in Pensacola to check out Fort Barrancas. I checked in through the gift shop, and learned I would have the fort all to myself. They had just opened for the day, it was off season and no other visitors were there yet. Fantastic I thought! This way I can really get a feel for the fort's history. The possibility of a ghostly encounter never even crossed my mind.

Entrance to the fort | Photo: Author

Fort Barrancas sits on a bluff overlooking Pensacola Bay. The location inspired engineers from Britain, Spain, and America to build forts here for almost 80 years. The British built the Royal Navy Redoubt here in 1763, the Spanish built two forts here in 1797. American engineers remodeled the battery in 1840, and started to build a masonry fort between 1839 and 1844, which was connected by an underground tunnel to the battery. The fort saw its first battle when Andrew Jackson took on the British, Spanish, and Creek Indians during the War of 1812. It was also the fort's first victory. The fort would see more action during the Civil War. Fort McRee, and Fort Barrancas were involved in an exchange of heavy cannon fire with Fort Pickens in late November 1861, and again in January 1862. By May 1862, the men stationed at the forts learned that the Union Army had taken New Orleans, the Confederate soldiers who were still stationed here abandoned Pensacola.

A Rare Sighting

Being something of a history buff; I would tour every square inch of the fort, and as I made my way around I found a narrow stair case that descended below ground. I followed it through a tunnel, and up another set of stairs. At the top of the stairs I discovered the area opened up into a long hallway that went to the left and the right. I discovered later that this area was known as the Counterscarp Gallery. It had a very strange feel to it, the barometric pressure dropped drastically. A terrifying sense of uneasiness swept over me. I have been a paranormal investigator for over 12 years, imagine how surprised I was at myself when this intense sensation kicked in my "fight or flight" response. Without thinking about it and before I realized it, I went down the steps I had just came up, back through the tunnel, then back up the steps and exited the fort. As I stood outside and collected myself, I started thinking, if it's haunted, it can't hurt me. I took a deep breath and headed back into the creepy hallway. As soon as I made it to the

5

The mysterious tunnel | Photo: Author

top of the steps, that eerie feeling came back. I was looking to my right down the long hall, when I suddenly felt something behind me. I turned around to see what was there. I was startled to see at the end of the long hall, the full body apparition of a Confederate Soldier looking at me from around the corner. I could clearly see that he was wearing a grey Confederate Uniform with a kepi atop his head, and holding a bayonet. He appeared to be approximately 6 feet tall, in his mid 40's, and appeared to have a partial beard. I looked right into his eyes; he nodded his head at me acknowledging my presence, and then vanished as he started to go back around the corner.

Doubting what I had seen, I headed quickly down the hallway and around the corner. There was no one there and nowhere for him to have gone! I had seen an apparition of a Confederate soldier! Hoping to lure the apparition into appearing again and interacting with me, I started talking to him and telling him about my relatives who were both in the Civil War. One had fought for the Confederacy, and the other for the Union. I also started talking about other things from that period. His image did not reappear, but I felt as if he were beside me as I walked alone through the entire fort. A detail I confirmed as I noticed I was casting two shadows, but one was about 6 feet tall, I knew it was the soldier's and not mine.

When I got back to the gift shop, I asked the woman who was working in the gift shop behind the counter, if they were allowed to talk about ghosts. I had barely posed the question when a man came from around the cubicle and said, "Tell me your story, then I will tell you mine!" I proceeded to tell them about the uneasy feeling and how I'd just seen a soldier, who seemed to follow me (judging by the extra shadow) throughout the fort. After I finished my story, the two employees told me that many people reported hearing things and seeing shadows. Some even felt a presence, but only a very few had actually seen him. The park ranger, who was also present, elaborated by adding the detail that the soldier was one of two who were executed on the grounds, according to legends, they were hung for falling asleep while on guard duty.

The Park Rangers didn't have a name for the soldier. This only made him more intriguing and I vowed to return in the future to see if I could communicate with him, and ask him who he is and why he is still lingering there? Maybe he feels compelled to guard the fort, since he was caught not doing his job. I have yet to make it back to Fort Barrancas, but I am extremely glad I got the brief experience to see this apparition, especially since he doesn't make himself known to everyone. My brief experience at the fort left me convinced that there was more to the story of this ghost and the fort.

FAMOUS GUESTS AND FRIENDLY GHOSTS AT THE INN
Florida House Inn, Fernandina

Fernandina's Historic Florida House Inn

Photo: Author

A Celebrated History

Everyone needs a place to stay when out of town. The Florida House Inn remains one of Florida's historic gems. The Inn was built in 1857 by David Yulee and during its early years was a boarding house for the railroad workers. During the Civil War the region was seized by the North and during that time, the Inn served as a boarding house to the Union Officers. After the war ended, the house was bought by a Major Leddy and his wife in 1865. They added a dining room and additional living space.

In 1882, ownership of the house passed to a Mrs. Joseph Higgins. While she owned the home, she added on yet again and that area now serves as an 8 room guest house. The house now boasts 16 guest rooms, an English Pub, a parlor, and a breakfast room. Over the years some highly celebrated names have stayed here. General Ulysses S. Grant, Jose Marti, The Carnegies, Rockefellers, Mary Pickford, and Henry Ford are just a few of the famous guests who have laid their heads to rest here. Perhaps these celebrities and temporary guests experienced the presence of a couple of resident ghosts lodging here on a more permanent basis?

7

The Inn's Resident Ghosts

One of the spirits rumored to still be residing at the Inn is a female who was said to have been murdered here. The story that I was told, described her as a madam who was brutally murdered here (possibly by a potential client). She is reportedly seen roaming through the house from time to time possibly still seeking her murderer or hoping they were captured.

There is also a tall morose man seen walking the hallways periodically. He is said to be searching for his beloved young wife who died during child birth at the Inn. Those who encountered him in most reports described him as very depressed and heartbroken. He has been seen all throughout the house and has a deep look of sorrow on his face.

Neither of the spirits reported at the Inn seem to interact with anyone. Most paranormal experts believe these types of repeating occurrences to be the result of residual energy trapped here from tragic deaths or occurrences. The tragedies described in the stories I researched, if true, may have left an impression on several rooms of the Inn and the atmosphere of the whole building. Still, when I visited the Inn, I felt there was nothing to be frightened of here, and it is a definite stop if you are in Fernandina. The Florida House Inn provides fans of the paranormal with rich history, great food, and ghost stories to talk about over lunch.

8

THE SUPERNATURAL SOLDIERS OF FT. CLINCH
Fort Clinch , Fernandina Beach

A History of Strong Defense
Defend the people! This was an idea that caused early U.S. settlements to build forts to protect their people and ports. Fort Clinch, on the peninsula of the northern-most point of Amelia Island is one of these historic battlements. The Fort looks over the entrance to Cumberland Sound and the Amelia River. Construction of the fort began after the end of the Seminole War in 1847. Like another famous military stronghold, it is pentagonal in shape with inner and outer walls, and consists of nearly five million bricks. There is a two story barracks in the center of the fort.

A view of Fort Clinch   Photo: Author

Fort Clinch was named in honor of General Duncan Lamont Clinch who died in 1849 and was a very important man in the first and second Seminole Wars. He also fought in the War of 1812. The fort was seized in 1861 by Confederate soldiers and provided a safe harbor for the Confederates during the beginning of the Civil War. It was recaptured by Federalist Army in early 1862 which gave the Union control of the Georgia and Florida coasts. The fort was also used in 1898 during the Spanish-American War, but was abandoned shortly after until the 1930's when the Civil Conservation Corps took it over and restored it.

The Noisy Fort, Re-enactors and Haunted Soldiers
Fort Clinch, like many restored Civil War forts is open to the public. Many visitors have reported hearing voice, footsteps, and all the other daily sounds you would have normally heard at a fort during the Civil War. Even more reports come from re-enactors who have spent the night at the fort or on its grounds. Many of whom claim the fort is definitely haunted! All of the re-enactors I have interviewed say the fort is pretty eerie at night. Sounds can be heard all around you. Shadowy figures are often seen out of the corner of your eye. According to the elements in these reports and their detailed stories about the frequent appearance of full blown apparitions, the fort would appear to be a very active place. One man I talked with told me that it was early in the morning (around 4 or 5am) when he awoke to a man standing over him and looking down at him. He was wearing a Federalist uniform and had his hands clasped in front of him. When the re-enactor acknowledged the man, he disappeared, an apparent

9

apparition. Another re-enactor told me that he was patrolling the grounds in Civil War garb when he noticed a misty figure at one of the end of the tunnels. His first thought was that someone was in there smoking. He decided he was going to walk up and say something to the smoker. However, as soon as he got close to the misty figure, it too vanished. Another common report was that of a Union soldier still walking the grounds looking for his wife. A tale told of a soldier who promised his wife nothing would happen to him and he would return to see her. He died before he could return to her and some say he is still walking the grounds of the fort looking for her or awaiting her arrival.

When I visited and walked around the fort researching my book, I felt as if someone were right on my heels the entire time. Everywhere I went I kept turning around because I literally thought someone was following me. I repeatedly heard the footsteps of someone coming up on me. I never saw anyone or anything out of the ordinary, but I am certain, in some way, I wasn't alone. The more I walked around, the more it became clear to me that Fort Clinch is an amazing place, whose past seems to echo and ripple even to this day. I felt a strong sense of curiosity and duty in this landmark spot of the War Between the States.

10

MURDER AT THE MARINA
Marina Seafood Restaurant, Fernandina Beach
....

Marina Seafood Restaurant at night

Photo: Author

The History of the Customs House

The Fernandina area of Florida is a magical place that has drawn many people over time to make it their home. One such person was Major William B. C. Duryee, who served with the Union Army Occupational Forces in Fernandina during the Civil War. He returned to Fernandina after the war and bought a piece of property where he began to build. He built a two story masonry structure, which was finished in the mid-1880s.

Originally built as a store selling hay, grain, and oats, the property began to be used for several purposes. The building housed the very first US Customs House (which occupied the building until the early 1900's). At one time, it also housed the oldest newspaper in the state, and the first Bank of Florida. The upstairs meanwhile, was used as a boarding house during the transformations taking place in the lower portion of the building.

After the Customs House relocated, the downstairs was converted into a restaurant and still exists today as the Marina Seafood Restaurant. The restaurant is considered by diners and many "foodies" to be the best food in town (I can vouch for that)! The upstairs is no longer a boarding house, but is used as office space for the restaurant and as an attorney's office.

Spirited Happenings Upstairs

The office in the middle of the upstairs (facing the main street) seems the most active and gives off very strange vibes. It is creepy enough that the manager of Marina Seafood Restaurant won't even enter the room unless there's no other choice. The attorney who is occupying part of the upstairs even went so far as to have the upstairs blessed trying to quiet things down a bit.

Reports of other disturbances include the eerie sounds of a dog whining heard up in the front office area by more than one witness. This is very strange since there are no dogs in the entire building. In fact, no evidence has been discovered to even suggest a dog ever being there.

One day a man was standing out on the street and looked up at the window because he noticed movement, there in the window, he saw two women primping and getting ready for a period style ball. He went into the restaurant to ask if there was a special reenactment event going on in town. The woman in the restaurant informed him there was no such event going on and that there was no one upstairs. The eyewitness repeat-

11

ed that he had clearly seen two women getting ready, so the man followed several of the employees upstairs, however, no one could be found anywhere in the entire upstairs area.

I spoke extensively to the manager, who has worked at the restaurant for 30 years. She believed the paranormal activity had been going on for at least 14 years. Sometimes, she will be in her office working and will clearly hear the door slam shut, Several times she has heard this and each time she will go out to see who could have so forcibly closed the door and there will be no one there. She even ruled out the idea of a gust of wind or blast of air conditioning. In addition, she told me that the dish washer upstairs periodically opens and slams shut on its own. She also mentioned that at one point in time dishes used to come off the shelf on their own accord and shatter on the floor. This doesn't seem to happen anymore, since the restaurant workers asked the spirits to stop breaking things.

Is a Tragic Betrayal the Source?

In my research efforts I came across several stories related to the building, but the one that I kept coming back to might best help explain the activity. This one tragic story attached to the building, featured a tragic act of betrayal and murder. Many years ago, when the upstairs was still a boarding house, a man had left his wife one morning to head to work. He almost made it to work before realizing he had forgotten something very important that he needed for the day. He turned around and headed home. When he arrived he discovered to his surprise, his wife, in bed with another man. He went into a fit of rage and killed them!

Maybe the angry husband's rage is the cause of the negative energy still lingering here. The sight of the murder that supposedly took place was the front room, where most visitors report experiencing unsettling and uncomfortable feelings. During my visit, certain areas of the marina gave me a vaguely unsettling feeling as well. Fortunately, these areas are situated in a completely different part of the building from the delicious Marina Restaurant. If you are in Fernandina, you need to stop by and enjoy a fabulous meal at the Marina. The friendly staff is very accommodating, and maybe you'll even have your own ghostly experience (if not try the dessert).

THE SORROWFUL BEACON
Amelia Island Lighthouse, Amelia Island

Amelia Island Lighthouse   Photo: Author

A Bright Past

Just as Amelia Island has served many masters, so too has her lighthouse. In 1820, a lighthouse was built on Cumberland Island, Georgia which is located off the Georgia and Florida coast. In 1838, the Cumberland Island lighthouse was dismantled, brick by brick, and shipped across the St. Marys River to be reconstructed on Amelia Island, the northernmost barrier island on Florida's Atlantic Coast. The highest spot on Amelia Island was chosen to allow the beacon to be much more visible.

In 1856, the light was upgraded from 14 lamps to a third order Fresnel lens. In 1861, the lighthouse was taken out of service due to the Civil War. When the war ended the lighthouse was put back into service.

In the 1930s, the light was electrified, and in 1970 it was automated, making it unnecessary for a light keeper to climb the 69 granite steps every day. This ended a long history of service for a line of devoted light keepers and their families. As most lighthouses do, Amelia Island Lighthouse, with its long history of service, has a few ghost stories attached to it as well.

The Sadness in the Tower

According to most of my research, a former light keeper and his beautiful bride are still reported to be haunting this lovely beacon. She allegedly died a tragic death, and unable to handle the loss of his beautiful bride, he killed himself by plummeting from the top of the light tower. Reports abound of sorrowful noises heard moving along as if climbing to the top of the tower. These reports then claim to hear the sound of the door opening and closing, and then an eerie silence. A feeling of sadness has been felt by many in the tower and additionally, cold spots are felt throughout. Is this another possible example of a residual haunting? Perhaps the light keeper dutifully replays his final tragic moments of life. As if to answer that question, the other frequent activity reported is that of a woman in a long flowing dress seen in and around the tower. She is believed to be the light keeper's wife.

My own experiences with the light house are limited and not as extensive as those in many of the reports I've researched (but I hope to rectify that soon). Still, Amelia Island Lighthouse is a beautiful tower with an interesting story of relocation and reconstruction, but with such a sadness attached to it. The touching story of the light keeper and his bride is suggestive of many similar stories at other lighthouses. Stories of light keepers who were so dedicated to their job of keeping sailors and the coast line safe and so attached to their duties of keeping the beacons, that even after their deaths many of their spirits are still keeping watch!

13

THE BASTARD PIRATE
AND THE BLOODY REPRISAL
Old Jail, Amelia Island

Behind Bars in Amelia Island

Amelia Island, Florida is no stranger to interesting history. In fact, it is often known as the "Isle of Eight Flags" for the eight different countries that once controlled it and flew their different flags here. In its rich history, it has seen captains and cutthroats, nobles and nasties come through its port. One of the oldest structures still standing on the island (and one that has seen its own fair share of law breakers and criminals) is the Old Jail. When a new jail was built in 1979, the old jail was in major disrepair. The County Commission offered the building to the Museum of History with a 99 year lease at only one penny per year. Thus the old jail on Amelia Island became the Amelia Island Museum of History. The museum is an interesting place full of local history from the Timucua Native Americans to the Spanish and French Explorers.

The building itself still has the jailhouse look on the outside, but doesn't look so much like it on the inside. It has been renovated for the museum, a gift shop, and office space. There is however, one area revealing the building's colorful past, where you can actually shut the doors on one cell and see what it must have felt like to have that door slam shut on you. Of course, it's a little different knowing you can just open the door and head home, but it still has a pretty interesting feel to it.

The Haunting History of a Pirate

The most interesting ghost story attached to the building and the grounds that was told to me during my research, was that of the bastard son of pirate Luis Aury. This pirate's "bastard son" was a major part of Amelia Island history. Luc Simone Aury, by name, he was a pirate just like his father, but much worse. Besides the crime of piracy, he was wanted for murder, rape, robbery, and many other offenses. After committing many horrific crimes, Luc was finally captured. He was sentenced to hang the day after his trial at the gallows behind the jail. The town was a buzz. There would soon be a hanging and people started making preparations to be there for the event. Most of the town appeared ready to attend Luc Aury's death.

Spiteful Luc, however, had other ideas. He wasn't going to have people gather around and watch him hang. He decided that night that he would slit his own throat instead, depriving the city of its chance to see him die a humiliating death. The police found him soon after he'd slit his throat, still alive, but barely. They summoned a surgeon, who quickly arrived and stitched up Aury's throat. The surgeon did all he could to keep the prisoner alive until the following morning, just long enough to hang him.

The following morning Luc Aury was prepared for the gallows with a high collared shirt buttoned to the top to cover the stitches. Barely able to stand, he was helped to the top of the gallows. The noose was tied around his neck and the hanging commenced. The trap door was sprung and as Aury's body dropped, the stitches ripped open nearly decapitating him. Luc managed one last spiteful act as his blood spewed

14

Amelia Island's Old Jail

Photo: Author

into the crowd. Some people fainted while others ran in fear at this horrific site.

Haunting Reports of the Gallows and My Experiences

The bulk of the reports of ghostly activity here are the fearful sounds of moaning, not a normal moan, but a gurgled moan from where the gallows once stood and inside the jail at night. Many people believe this is the sounds of Luc Aury, who with his throat slit and stitched up, could have been moaning in pain while choking on his own blood. Other reports consist of a male apparition with stitches in his throat or with his collar buttoned practically all the way up to his chin.

Unfortunately, I was only able to visit the museum during the day. During my research I didn't see or hear anything that matched the reports, but I did feel a great sense of agony behind the building. It wasn't until I had concluded my visit and continued my research that I discovered this was where the gallows once stood.

GLOWING EYES AND GHOSTLY HYMNS
Kingsley Plantation, Fort George Island

It's a long road leading to Kingsley Plantation. At the start you feel as if you are driving through the middle of nowhere on this swampy, forest-lined road. As you continue traveling, the road becomes long, winding and narrow. The farther you progress on that dirt road back to Kingsley Plantation, the more you have that eerie feeling that someone is watching you. The deeper you get into the woods, the more the feeling grows and the sensation that your "viewers" are growing in numbers. Who are they? Where are they? Why can't you see any of them!

Kingsley Plantation   Photo: Author

The Indian Plague

Back in the 1700's, when the Europeans were moving here to start a new life (and taking the land away from the Timucua Indians), this long, winding road was actually the sight where the mission, the Europeans built, once stood. There are no remnants of the mission, just stories told in the oral tradition that have been passed down.

Unfortunately, as the new settlers traveled here, they also brought with them disease. As the settlers came in contact with the Indians, the disease spread, wiping out the entire tribe! There are no descendants of the Timucua Indians.

Seeing Red

There are many reports of people driving down this road at night and seeing red eyes in the woods peering out at them and following them down the path. The closer you get to Kingsley Plantation, the more eyes start to appear in the woods watching you. Many people believe that when you're driving down this road it is the ghosts of the Indians who are watching you, wondering perhaps if more settlers are coming to do more damage to their tribe and land.

The Plantation's Revolutionary History

As you travel farther down the road to Kingsley Plantation, you will eventually come upon a gate that is the main entrance. The main house, nearby, was built in 1793, by John McQueen, who acted as a courier for General George Washington during the Revolutionary War. He ordered his slaves to build their living quarters on the site where you see them today. Continuing through the gate, and looking to your left or your right you'll see the still standing slave shacks. There are 25 of the original 32 coquina shacks still here.

Eventually the slave shacks and the plantation itself would come into the possession of John McIntosh of Woodbine, Georgia. He bought the plantation from McQueen in 1804, when McQueen became heavy in debt (due to bad weather) and had trouble getting his crops to grow. McIntosh lived here with his family and was a successful planter. In fact, he was one of the wealthiest planters in the province.

In 1817, McIntosh sold the plantation to Zephaniah Kingsley for the price of $7,000 (a bargain price at the time). The Kingsley's slaves restored the main house and the slave quarters and built a barn on the property.

In 1806, Zephaniah sailed to Cuba to bring back slaves for his plantation. While there he purchased a 13 year old girl by the name of Anta Majigeen Ndiaye. She was from Senegal, a country in West Africa. When they arrived back in Florida, he introduced her as Anna and told people they had been married in a foreign land by native African customs. Within the next 5 years she and Zephaniah had 3 children, and in 1811, when she turned 18, Kingsley (in a move considered revolutionary for the time) freed Anna and their three children. Anna had gone from an African Princess, to a Florida slave and eventually to a Plantation and slave owner.

Old Ruins | Photo: Author

My Personal Experiences

As you walk through the ruins, you can't help but become attuned to who was there and all that they went through. Day after day working for the plantation owner and not having anything much to show for it except abuse and hopes of the chance to one day become free. As I roamed my way in and out of the coquina ruins, I could hear the faint sound of someone humming. It sounded almost like an old hymn. I started to look around, trying to figure out where it was coming from and realized there was no one else around. I continued my visit through the old ruins, when the sounds of humming increased. I got the sensation that there was more than one person humming and it seemed to be getting a little louder. I couldn't help but wonder, as I made my way farther through the slave quarters, if perhaps some of them were still here, tending to their homes and their daily chores. I tried to talk with them, letting them know they could be at peace now. There was no one to keep them, or enslave them anymore. The humming seemed to grow more at ease. I told them they could go on now; there was no reason for them to still be hanging around here. I continued back to my car and the humming became fainter, as if it was down to one person, just as it was when I first heard it.

When I had reached the gift shop, one of the rangers greeted me and I asked her about the humming I heard near the slave quarters. She looked surprised. She responded with, "You heard it too?" She told me many people had reported hearing old hymns being hummed around the slave shacks. The ranger also told me that many people, who said they'd been out there at night, have seen apparitions walking around the slave quarters. In fact, other visitors have reported seeing Anna herself, walking the grounds near the slave quarters and especially in the kitchen building (where her living quarters were coincidentally located). Anna's ghost has been seen in the main house as well. I enjoyed my conversation with the ranger, and hope to return to Kingsley Plantation (just as Anna seems to) and explore this historic state area further.

HAUNTINGS ON THE MENU
Copper Top Restaurant, Jacksonville Beach
....

Alpha's Place

There's no place like home. In this case, it's Alpha Paynter's home. Alpha Paynter was the original owner of a historically rich pine log home built in 1934. Mrs. Paynter's place served as a boarding house and adoptive home for orphans, until it became a restaurant in 1947 (serving southern home style cooking).

Alpha sold the building to Preban and Nina Johansen in 1962, and they in turn, sold to Carmen Macri. The home has had several owners since then, and was known for years as the "Homestead Restaurant" (a fixture in Jacksonville Beach until its closing). Today, it has been renovated and reborn as the delicious Copper Top Restaurant. Despite many owners coming and going over the years, eyewitnesses claim there is one previous owner that is definitely still here, and that is Alpha.

Ms. Paynter's in the House

Many witnesses have claimed to see Ms. Paynter near the fireplace (the oldest part of the house) located in the center of the restaurant. Some have reportedly even heard her humming as if she was tending the fireplace, still trying to keep her home warm on chilly nights. There have also been reports of Ms. Paynter's ghost appearing in the ladies room. Many of these reports detail accounts of witnesses seeing a woman in the mirror behind them or seeing a shadow in a part of the room where a shadow wouldn't normally be cast. When I visited the Copper Top researching this book I shared the same experience commonly found in these eyewitness accounts and one that convinced me this was no trick of the lights! While washing my hands alone in the ladies room, I noticed a shadow at the other end of the room, in an area without a reasonable light source to have cast it. Upon noticing the shadow, I stopped, purposely remaining motionless, and verifying that I wasn't accidentally the cause. The shadow, however, continued to move until it eventually and gradually faded out. Other visitors to the restaurant have even reported that besides the shadow, a presence -many believe to be Alpha - putting its hand on their shoulder or stroking their hair while they are in the rest room. Although I never encountered these other situations myself, the experiences I did have, gave me a greater appreciation for the plausibility of their stories and accounts.

In addition to the fireplace and rest room, Alpha has also been seen on the landing at the top of the stairs and walking the hallway on the second floor. In these instances her appearance is often accompanied by voices and whispers, but listeners can never quite make out what is being said. None of the reports I researched indicated that Alpha was trying to frighten people. In fact, most eyewitnesses were more startled by her unexpected appearance than anything else.

Alpha's Active Roommates

Records indicate that a young boy passed away in Alpha's place when it was being run as an adoption home. He is said to often play with the water. I spoke to one of the

18

current owners of the restaurant about these "water stories" and he told me about one of his own personal experiences. He was alone, upstairs in the building at night doing renovations to prepare another area for the Copper Top's opening. He decided to be brave and ask if anything was there in the building with him. Suddenly, in the middle of the bathroom renovation area (where he was standing), the water in the shower came on, water that wasn't even connected! He said it startled him enough to make him stop working for the night and go home.

The kitchen crew has also reported unusual water activity and the lights turning on and off by themselves. Employees have also mentioned dishes that have been known to slide straight off the shelf and float out into midair, before crashing to the floor. Further, there have been several times when they have come in early to prep for the day, only to find shattered dishes all over the floor and menus scattered around the hostess station.

There have been other reports of activity that employees of the Copper Top do not believe to be Alpha. According to the employees and their experiences, Alpha is respectable and still considers this her home. Legend states that Alpha is buried in the backyard, but records indicate that she was cremated. Regardless, she seems to prefer things to be tidy and proper. They don't believe she would do anything mischievous or destructive, and are not really sure who is still lingering and doing the damage. If these unusual activities are not the spirited work of a mischievious male child, then perhaps some of the other legends attached to the house might shed some light on the culprits.

In the 1960's, a woman reportedly committed suicide by hanging herself in the back of the restaurant. Ten years later, stories claim that her daughter hung herself here too, in what is now the storage closet. No one seems to know who the women were or why they killed themselves, but they weren't alone. Another story mentions a man who hung himself from a rope where the back porch used to be. A negative person, he had supposedly had enough, he wrapped the noose around his neck and aggravated, kicked out the chair from underneath himself, dyeing on the property like the others.

Whether this man is truly the main entity responsible for the destructive paranormal activity, or part of a group of ghosts "rooming" in the house, remains to be seen. No reports of anyone being harmed here surfaced during my research (although admittedly some of the records are a little spotty). Instead, I followed up on the many cases of eyewitnesses who were just a little unnerved or shocked, and if they were in the wrong room during these manifestations perhaps a little messy. One thing is certain, however, this is a great "historic haunt" with absolutely fabulous food, and great history. Visitors to the Copper Top may experience Alpha, or some of these things themselves, but at the very least, they will have some great ghost stories to tell over dinner.

APARTMENTS AND APPARITIONS
St. John's Landing Apartments, Green Cove Springs

Housing Military

The buildings that run along the St. Johns River in Green Cove Springs were originally built as military housing in the 1930's, but are now known as the St. John's Landing Apartments. One strange thing about this housing complex is the cemetery located in the middle. When the military base closed, the buildings were sold to a private owner. Over the years they fell into disrepair and eventually became low rent housing. In 1997, new owners took over, and restored all the buildings to their original appearance. They are now being rented out again.

It's Not Just the Wind!

There have been an abundant amount of paranormal reports here. When I ventured out to find these buildings, the only thing I knew was that they were reported to be haunted, they were used as military housing, and that there was a cemetery somewhere on the property (or so my research told me). With only these basics, I decided to experience the site myself before I waded through the eyewitness reports. I pulled into the complex and started looking for the location of the cemetery. This seemed like a good place to start. As soon as I saw the cemetery and pulled up in front of it, I had a strange feeling. It felt as if there were people all around me, watching me. I am not a paranoid person, but that distinct feeling of several people around me was getting stronger the longer I was there. As I walked up to the locked gate of the cemetery, I felt the temperature drop by at least 10 degrees, and the K2 EMF meter began going off like crazy. I didn't feel a particular person or spirit wanting to communicate with me, but there definitely was something around!

As I walked the perimeter of the cemetery, I kept turning around looking behind me and in several directions because I still had the feeling I wasn't alone. My activity at the cemetery drew the attention of one resident who I had the chance to interview. The man had lived there many years and claimed to have the same sense of being watched around the cemetery. As I continued investigating, I learned that other residents had heard voices in their apartments. They described to me hearing whispered conversations constantly, but never quite being able to make out what was being said. These instances occurred when radios, televisions, and appliances were off, and their neighbors were gone on either side. It made the source of these phantom noises even more mysterious.

Other residents reported footsteps, and doors opening and closing on their own. I also came across reports of kitchen cabinets opening and slamming shut as if by unseen hands. Additional reports detailed full body apparitions, and shadow figures, seen throughout the complex (especially around the cemetery). Eyewitnesses even claimed that cold spots are felt all around, inside and outside of the apartments and a multitude of reports of electrical charges in the air, again, frequently around the cemetery! Water is a major conductor for the paranormal and the entire property is along the St. Johns River. This could be one reason why there is so much paranormal activity here. In all of my research involving the St. John's Landing Apartments, I came across none of the usual instances of tragedy or traumatic events that seem to lead to these types of paranormal activity. That makes the large number of reports even more baffling. Whether the activity stems from the cemetery in the center, or something else in the complex, it's hard to ignore the reports. Until more details become available, it's easy to declare this site a "Historic Haunt".

The cemetery and St. John's Landing Apartments   Photo: Author

21

GHOSTLY SURPRISES BREWING AT THE FORMER "HOUSE OF WAX"

A1A Ale Works, St. Augustine

The Surprise

How do you shop when the store's products are a mystery to you? That was the dilemma early shoppers in the building now known as A1A Ale Works faced. In the mid 1800's, when the structure was originally built, there was a strong need for a store to receive unloaded merchandise from the boats when they arrived in port. Without the modern conveniences of phones or emails to let them know a shipment was coming, and how long it would remain fresh; the decision was made to build a store close to the docks (so when perishable items arrived they wouldn't spoil before they made it to the store shelves). Thus, the aptly named "Surprise Department Store" was born, with customers surprised to find they could be receiving fish and fabrics in the same shipment.

Unfortunately, the only place available to build a store of this kind was on the corner of what are now King and Marine Streets. This presented a problem. The area was already a catholic cemetery. Instead of moving all the bodies, they decided to build the building 3 feet above the ground, above the graves. They thought this would be more respectful. At the time when the store was located here there were glass panels in the floor allowing you to actually look down and see the graves!

The Infamous "House of Wax"

After the department store moved out, Potter's Wax Museum moved in. Established in 1948, it became the first Wax Museum in the United States and the company became one of the city's biggest tourist draws (turning the heads of many St. Augustine skeptics who weren't sure if the endeavor would succeed). Potter's Wax Museum drew visitor's and fan's attention to the

Early postcard

Author's Collection

attraction, the building and the city, and became a St. Augustine fixture. Besides St. Augustine, the Wax Museum would draw Hollywood's attention too. In the 1950's, the famous film "The House of Wax" starring Vincent Price was reputed to be inspired by and contain a trailer and several scenes filmed at the museum. Further, surprisingly enough, more than 20 films have been produced in whole or in part in St. Augustine, with actors like Gary Cooper, William Hurt, and Rob Lowe. Many of these celebrities would eventually find themselves immortalized in George Potter's museum. These iconic Hollywood celebrities and the many others depicted in wax, helped give Mr. Potter a reputation as a successful local businessman; while those who worked for him knew he seriously cared for his employees. When any of his store or museum clerks were closing alone; he had a habit of coming down to the store and staying with them until they finished for the night and could get safely home. Potter's museum was eventually moved a few doors down from its original spot years later, and the building, after seeing many businesses, has since been renovated and revamped into several store fronts and the very popular A1A Ale Works.

Welcome Back Potter

Apparently Mr. Potter's spirit is still believed to be lingering in the building late at night when employees are closing up. He still comes back to his original building and has been reported on more than one occasion at the current location as well. Most of the reports I researched involved people feeling a very comforting presence and hearing footsteps behind them. The witnesses never seemed scared, occasionally a little startled, but there seems to be nothing to be afraid of when Mr. Potter is around.

More Spirits Brewing

There are other spirits believed to be haunting the A1A Ale Works besides that of Mr. Potter, but no one knows for sure who they might be. The employees and others describe a very active upstairs bar at night. Typically when all the customers have left and there are only one or two people left in the restaurant. Employees report putting all the chairs and bar stools up on the table, blowing candles out, and trying to complete closing duties. They usually leave the main bar and continue closing other areas before often hearing a huge commotion. When they return to the dining room or bar area, all the chairs are back on the floor, candles are lit, and the tables are set.!

Based on my interviews and research, I don't believe the spirit or spirits in the upstairs bar area are Mr. Potter. He has no attachment to the restaurant, and the reported behavior is drastically different from those described by other eyewitnesses. Who could it be then? Maybe it's a former worker of the restaurant; or perhaps someone buried below. Besides redecorating, this spirit never seems to interact with anyone, so we may never learn its identity.

Besides the paranormal activity in the upstairs bar, the microbrewery also boasts reports of a female apparition seen on the back staircase. Local legends state that on her wedding day she was to descend the stairs in her wedding dress. It goes on to say she made it halfway before she fell to her death, breaking her neck on the back stair case. Her apparition has been seen and described by many, coming down the steps, and vanishing half way down. Even some of the local ghost tour guides have had unexpected sightings here. When I visited this area I felt a great heaviness and sadness, like those experienced by many I spoke to.

The heavy, uneasy, or unusual feelings associated with this building are not limited to the areas most visitors and employees see. I spoke with a construction crew member who has had to do some work under the building (since there are pipes and wires below the building). He described a strong, uneasy feeling, coming over him whenever he had to go under the building. He claimed crawling over all those graves just gives you a sense of desecration and disrespect. In fact, he has actually had a couple of crew members over the years quit after crawling under there and experiencing it themselves.

With all the detailed reports from eyewitnesses, employees, tourists, workers and others; it's very clear that the building has a history of some unusual activity. Even if you don't believe in these kinds of spirits, A1A Ale Works is worth a visit. Sporting a specialty collection of micro brews that are brewed on site at the restaurant; fans of the paranormal or just people seeking a good night out would do well to explore for themselves and grab a tasty pint.

THE SHADOWY AVIATOR
Airplane Graveyard, US1 St. Augustine

The Metal Graveyard

The metal graveyard was hard to miss. As you traveled down US1 heading towards St. Augustine you would see a small field containing 9 Grumman S2 Tracker military planes. Their metal husks lay in disrepair and made this odd collection resemble a plane junkyard. Most of the planes were from the 1960's and 1970's. The oldest plane on the lot was from 1964 or 65.

A resident of the graveyard Photo: Miles Minson

During their fighting years they were used for military operations, performing off shore reconnaissance. The planes were now being used for parts, to restore other old Grumman's that weren't in such bad shape. The graveyard was located on private property, in the middle of a fenced in area, but most locals new of a secret location where you could slide under the fence. The neighbors didn't seem to mind either, as long as you were quiet, and didn't bother them. And why wouldn't you want to see them; even if the planes weren't actively flying, they were still an impressive sight.

"Letting yourself in" to a private area so close to a nearby police station, however, was a dangerous proposition. Still, the lure of paranormal activity drew some die-hard fans to risk the danger. It became apparent as these fans and their stories circulated more and more frequently, that even if the planes were inactive, paranormal activity did take place. Many of these reports detailed the presence of a shadowy figure walking around the aircrafts late at night. According to these eyewitness accounts, you could never make out a face or any details, but you could tell it was a man, possibly one of the old pilots, or maybe one of the maintenance workers who worked on the planes.

Me and My Shadow

One night, I decided I was going to go out there and see for myself if the stories were true or just a local legend. When I arrived I found the spot under the fence that everyone had told me about and crawled inside. Unfortunately, I did not have my camera with me, but I did have my K2 EMF (Electro Magnetic Field) Meter in hand, I also thought to bring a cohort to help corroborate my experiences. As I slowly walked around all the planes, I noticed that the K2 gave me a strong energy reading around 2 of the planes in particular. The first appeared to have a bullet hole in the cockpit window on the left side of the plane. The plane gave off a very heavy feeling as I walked around it. I continued working my way around the area with my K2 meter and nothing

25

seemed to happen, until I came upon the second unusual plane, located in the dead center of the lot. This second plane gripped me with a feeling as if it were looking at me, or someone in it! I stared up at the plane and noticed my EMF meter starting to spike like mad. The lights went all the way up to the red. Immediately afterwards I looked towards the end of the plane. I could have sworn someone was there watching me. I saw nothing, but my meter continued to spike. I then asked, "is there anyone here?" At that point, I noticed something out of the corner of my eye. When I looked up, I saw him! There was a very tall shadowy figure of a man, easily over 6 feet tall with broad shoulders watching me from behind the tail end of the plane. This unexpected figure surprised and startled me.

To be totally honest, I thought the stories I had heard about the graveyard were just a legend, the product of overactive imaginations, but as I stared at this semi-transparent shadowy figure I knew they were real! I moved to the side to see if he would follow, and he did. As I moved he moved. This meant he was an intelligent haunt, because he knew I was there, and was interacting with me. I slowly moved towards the other side of the plane, the shadow followed me. We reached the tail at the end of the plane, my meter going off the entire time. It was very exciting. I just wish I had brought my camera with me to capture something besides the K2 readings.

Eventually, the shadowy figure retreated into the dark and I headed back towards the fence. I confirmed the erratic K2 behavior with my fellow ghost hunter, and we both felt energized and excited.

The Vanishing Graveyard

I decided midsummer of 2011 that I would go back to the graveyard and continue my investigation. To my surprise, the airplane graveyard was gone. All the planes had been hauled away and the lot was now being used for something else. Another Florida roadside interest gone and the mystery of the shadowy figure still unsolved.

26

THE PLACE IS HAUNTED, BELIEVE IT OR NOT

Castle Warden/ Ripley's Believe It Or Not Museum, St. Augustine

The Wardens, the Famous Author, and the Talented Mr. Ripley

Where do you keep a shrunken head, mummified cat, erector-set carousel, and two headed rabbit? That's the same question the famous Robert Ripley asked himself, until he discovered Castle Warden in St. Augustine. The talented Mr. Ripley had amassed quite a collection of the odd and unusual in his travels. Amazingly, after all the places he'd ventured, he had his heart set on housing his collection in this unique Moorish Revival structure. However, the building already boasted a colorful history long before Ripley became a frequent visitor in the 1940's.

Castle Warden

Photo Courtesy: Ralf Ingwerson, Ripley's Believe It Or Not

Before its current incarnation as Ripley's Believe it or Not Museum, it was known as Castle Warden. It was built in 1887, as the winter home of William G. Warden who was a business partner to John D. Rockefeller and Henry Flagler. One of the few known poured concrete castles from the 1800's, it remained in the family until the 1930's. In 1941, another noteworthy came into possession of Castle Warden, and remodeled it into a successful upscale hotel. The new owners, Pulitzer Prize winning author Marjorie Kinnan Rawlings (The Yearling) and her hotelier husband Norton Baskin, owned the "Castle Warden Inn" during the World War II era. It was during this time that Mr. Ripley became a frequent guest and admirer of the building. He tried unsuccessfully for several years to acquire it for his museum. Unfortunately, Ripley died in 1949. In December of 1950, his heirs honored his wishes and finally managed to buy the estate. This purchase, no doubt, made easier by a mysterious fire in the building in April of 1944 that caused the death of two women and extensive damage to Castle Warden. After the damage to the building was fixed, the accidental fire became and unfortunate memory and the country's very first Ripley's Believe it or Not Museum opened!

Marjorie Kinnan Rawlings

Photo Courtesy: Ralf Ingwerson, Ripley's Believe It Or Not

27

Mr. Ripley at Castle Warden

Photo Courtesy: Ralf Ingwerson,
Ripley's Believe It Or Not

The Burning Question

Was the fire really an accident?
Two women, Ruth Hopkins and
Betty Neville Richson were
believed to have died in the fire
here, but did they? Many now
believe they may both have been murdered before the fire was started, the blaze possibly providing a perfect way for the culprit to cover his tracks.

Investigators looking for a common link between the two women think it highly unlikely that the two ladies knew each other. Betty was in her 20's and had just checked in literally 90 minutes before the fire, and her death occurred. Unlike the new guest Betty, Ruth had been staying in the fourth floor penthouse apartment for some time, at the insistence of the hotel owner and her friend Marjorie Kinnan Rawlings. She was thought to be hiding from her highly abusive husband. Many people now believe that her husband found where she was hiding, came from their former residence a few blocks away and killed her, He is then believed to have killed Betty and started the fire trying to cover up the murder of his wife and any witnesses. We may never know the truth, but one thing we do know is the castle is full of paranormal activity, and it occurs on an almost daily and nightly basis.

The Women in the Windows and a Cold Hand in the Dark

Many people I interviewed described seeing two women looking out the windows of Betty and Ruth's rooms. If they are the apparitions of the two women who perished that day in the fire, perhaps they are looking for rescue or justice. Besides the reports of the two women, many people have reported being touched or hearing voices in the museum. The reports of paranormal activity in Castle Warden have persisted, and gathered enough attention to draw a crew and an investigation from a famous televised paranormal group. My employer, GhoSt Augustine, had been selling equipment earlier in the evening, and I was invited to join the investigations at the museum. It was an eventful and thoroughly enjoyable night with an amazingly talented crew.

Later in the evening I decided I would investigate a little more on my own. In my experiences, I have generally had more success in detecting and discovering paranormal activity with smaller groups. So I figured I would go off and find a quiet place to explore. I have always been drawn to the history of Egypt, and the mummified cat is my favorite exhibit in the building, so I decided to head there. When I got to the room where the mummified cat was, there was no one to be found. As I looked at the cat and wondered about the stories attached to it, I felt a hand on my shoulder. I was startled for a moment and turned to see who had come up behind me. I discovered to my surprise, that I was very much alone! This personal encounter was icing on the cake for a successful night with the paranormal group in Castle Warden.

Another of the common reports I've been told by visitors to Castle Warden, are that of mysterious voices in the building. These reports seemed even more believable after the paranormal investigators from the television show found EVPs while filming, However, my favorite story involving voice based paranormal activity at Castle Warden, was told to me by a friend, and the Ghost Tour Director at Ripley's, Ralf Ingwersen. Here is his story:

"On a rather non-descript night I was working late at my desk, oblivious to the time, when I suddenly realized the evening's ghost tours may very well have been completed, leaving me all alone in the building, leaving ME as the person who would have to make the final rounds and lock the old castle up for the night. Gulp. Let's face it. We all feel uncomfortable alone in the dark, in any building or place. Disney World after hours, in the dark, late at night? It would probably feel like the creepiest place on Earth rather than the happiest...

As I headed toward the main entrance to begin shutting off breakers and turning off lights, the thought struck me that the final tour may NOT have left the building. What if our guide Monica was still on the third floor with her group? Our original 1880's wooden staircases creak and groan with every step, so sneaking upstairs to check might have given guests the impression we stage or create effects to scare them on the ghost tour. We don't. So I chose to wait another moment or two in our "Pirate" room, out of sight, just in case the group was about to walk by. And then I heard her say my name. "Ralf", she said clearly.

My first thought was 'how in the heck did Monica get BEHIND me in this small room?' My second thought was 'Monica would NEVER sneak up on anyone and do that....ever."

I didn't have a third thought. I turned and looked, and, yes, I was still the only person in the room. My spine was tingling with energy and I felt a quick chill go through my body, a shudder, really. A heartbeat or two later, the rumbling sound of footsteps cascaded in from down the hall. These were coming from the limbs of the living, however, at least a score of souls, who, unlike whatever had uttered my name, were soon to leave the building. Monica and her group of about 25 guests had been on the third floor the whole time, and were just now happily thumping down the stairs, while I, frozen, simply wanted to run out of the building!

Not more than two minutes later, that's exactly what I did, neglecting my duties to canvas the second and third floors, knowing full well I'd get that 6:30 a.m. phone call from the following day's opening manager wondering why I didn't. After THAT? I simply couldn't."

Ralf's experience and those of many others, are the reasons why Ripley's is a must see for paranormal fans, and tourists alike. The most fantastic thing about the Ripley's Museum is that you can check out the history of the Castle and the mysteries of Robert Ripley by day, and then check out the ghosts by night. With over a century of rich stories behind it, Castle Warden is what I call a true "Historic Haunt".

THE GIRL AT THE GATE
St. Augustine City Gate, St. Augustine

The City Gate and the "Yellow Death"

Defend the town at all costs! The Spanish settlers of early St. Augustine were very concerned with the safety of their colony. Despite these concerns, St. Augustine was 150 years old before the decision was made to build walls around the city to protect it from attacks. An assault by the English in 1702 probably helped make the decision easier for the townsfolk. So in 1704, construction began on the Cubo Line which extended west from the fort on the north side of town. Along the Cubo Line was the main entrance into the town which eventually became known as the City Gate.

The Gate tourists see standing today is mainly constructed of coquina. Due to the deterioration of timber and earthworks, the walks and the gate were rebuilt several times. The last time it was rebuilt was 1808 this was the final reconstruction of the original gate on the Cubo Line. During the Second Seminole War (between 1835 and 1842) the wall protected the city from the Seminole Indians and their attempted invasion of St. Augustine.

The gate was guarded heavily, not just to keep out attacks, but disease as well. During the yellow fever epidemic the city relied on the gate to keep out sick people so they didn't infest the entire town. However, the gate didn't work as well at fighting off illness as it did invaders.

The Ghostly Greeting

The main paranormal tale involving the City Gate, centers on the main gate keeper and his daughter Elizabeth. Together they guarded the gate daily. Elizabeth always dreamed of being a gate-keeper, like her father. In fact, she wanted to be the first female gate keeper. Unfortunately, at the age of 13, young Elizabeth contracted yellow fever along with the rest of her family and died. But maybe her dream did come true. Many people have reported late night visions of a young girl waving to people at the City Gates as if she was welcoming them to town. Even local law enforcement officers have seen this ghostly image of a young girl in a light colored gown. The

An apparition caught at St. George Inn

Photo: Author

30

police department has responded to many calls detailing the appearance of a young girl in front of the gate (typically around 3 a.m.). These callers are deeply concerned because they truly believe they've seen a real person, a young girl alone in the early morning hours, not an apparition.

Elizabeth has also been repeatedly seen by witnesses around what is now the St. George Inn (located right across the street from the gate). She never seems to interact with anyone other than waving at them. Because she seems to be repeating the same motions time after time, many investigators believe she may just be residual energy.

During my own investigations I have seen Elizabeth's apparition frequently. In fact, I managed to capture a full body apparition one night with my camera. It is one of my favorite photos from a collection that includes many investigations.

Residual haunting or not, it looks as if young Elizabeth's dream came true and she did become the very first female gate keeper in St. Augustine. In fact, paranormal reports would seem to indicate that she is still here continuing to help guard this historic city.

*A blowup of one of
my favorite pictures,
the full body apparition
of Elizabeth at St. George Inn*

Photo: Author

31

A STUDY IN HISTORY AND GHOSTS
Ponce de Leon Hotel/ Flagler College, St. Augustine

Flagler and His Marvelous Hotel

Everyone enjoys a vacation! The idle rich are no exception. Railroad magnate Henry Flagler envisioned St. Augustine as the next vacation hot spot for the rich. The millionaire built Ponce de Leon Hotel to house these financially well-off guests. The hotel first opened on January 10th, 1888. In its heyday, it was known as the classiest hotel in town, and had one of the most modern amenities, electricity! The hotel was a concerted effort by some of the most talented people of its time. It was one of the

Flagler College　　Photo: Author

first poured concrete structures in the U.S., and due to Flagler's friendship with Thomas Edison, one of the first to enjoy electricity. Some interior areas of the hotel were credited to Louis Comfort Tiffany (whose glass works would later garner him worldwide fame). Other areas of the hotel were decorated by noted artisans who would later go on to supervise the World's Fair, and execute murals for the Library of Congress. The original twin towers of the hotel were water storage tanks, providing running water to hotel guests. Many notables stayed at the hotel during its years of service including Mark Twain, Theodore Roosevelt, Babe Ruth and many others.

During Flagler's time at the Ponce de Leon Hotel, he had a long history with women. He married three times and both his first and second wives died at very early ages (but there are several very interesting stories attached to his second wife Ida). Flagler's relationship is the subject of many contradictory reports. He was reputed to be a very devoted caregiver to his first wife. Flagler's relationship with his second and third wives seemed to raise many eyebrows in the polite society of the time.

Flagler had power, and enough of it in fact, to put his second wife Ida, away in a mental hospital with very little effort. According to some reports from the time, Ida's behavior was occasionally extreme for women of that age, which may have contributed to Flagler's decision. In one account, Ida reportedly entered the Men's bar one night (now the snack room) slightly inebriated and embarrassed her husband greatly. Only men were allowed in this room, and her "barging-in" drunk, sent him into a rage. As a result of this incident, he reportedly locked her in the mirror door room. Stories claim this entrapment contributed to her being driven insane and her subsequent admission to a mental hospital. Some reports from the time would suggest that she didn't really go crazy, but may have been going through extremes of menopause.

32

Flagler not wanting to deal with her emotions and hormones, or not understanding the nature of menopause, sent her away. That made his marriage to his third wife very convenient. Reports of the hotel being haunted never surfaced until after Flagler's death in 1913. After his passing, Flagler's body was put on display for the viewing of family and friends and many, many people attended. He was a prominent figure in the development of Florida and St. Augustine.

World War II and the "Lost Colony"

During World War 11, the hotel was adapted to become a Coast Guard training center (many people consider it to be the birthplace of the Coast Guard Reserve). It was also around this time that the government implemented several programs to revitalize the tourism industry. Several high profile authors were known to have visited, worked, or lived in St. Augustine at the time and all of them reportedly admired the hotel. This "lost colony" of artists included noteworthies like Ernest Hemingway, Zora Neale Hurston, Robert Frost, and Marjorie Kinnan Rawlings.

The Coming of Civil Rights and a New College

In the early 60's, St. Augustine became one of the lesser known, but highly influential sites of the civil rights movement. Drawing many protestors to the city and the hotel (the incidents and events were reported in the New York Times and brought Martin Luther King into town among others). In 1968, the hotel was converted into a large part of the newly-established Flagler College. In 1975, it was added to the U.S. National Register of Historic Places, and in 2006 became a U.S. National Historic Landmark.

The Ghosts of the College

Few stories or reports of paranormal activity exist from the hotel's early days. One of the most popular involves a janitor's activities shortly after Flagler's death. The janitor came through the building and thought to himself how disrespectful it was for all the windows and doors to be open during Mr. Flagler's funeral. As he went through the hotel, he began closing all the doors and windows. He reached the last door in the rotunda, and shut it. Legends claim that Flagler's spirit was trying to escape and it hit the door and bounced back, and settled into one of the tiles in the rotunda room's floor. (A common belief back in the day was that during a funeral, windows should be left open so the soul of the deceased could escape this world and go on to the next). There is a faint image of a face in this tile with only a passing resemblance to Henry Flagler. Still, Flagler's ghost is often seen throughout the college. Many individuals claim to have seen a rather tall,

The face in the tile Photo: Author

slender man walking around in a dark suit, hat, and cane. The descriptions given by these eyewitnesses match that of Mr. Flagler.

Many of the other reports of paranormal activity seem to focus not on Mr. Flagler, but on his wife Ida. Many stories have surfaced which would seem to suggest that while Ida Alice was staying at the hotel, she might have been trying to conjure up the dead herself. She was known to play with Ouija boards and dabbled in the supernatural. Many of the paranormal reports gathered over the years, detailing Ida and other activity come from Flagler College students. I know several former Flagler College students personally and some have shared their stories with me. One student detailed an experience involving another girl, whose room was neighboring the room where Ida Alice, Flagler's second wife, reportedly still haunts the college to this day. It is also reported to be the legendary room where Flagler's mistress supposedly hung herself. College students have reportedly peeked through the key hole, and seen the vision of a woman hanging from a noose in this room. No one is allowed in this room. It was used strictly for storage and reportedly still is.

The woman I spoke with shared stories with me about banging coming from the adjoining wall. Her room shared a common wall with this most haunted room in the college. Things would violently fall off that wall and land on the floor, but would never break. She also described banging at different times of the day and night when no one was in the other room. Even the radio would turn itself on when it was on the shelf next to the haunted room. When she moved the radio to the other side of her room it would work properly and she never had any problems with it.

Another common paranormal report from the college occurs in the hallway where the Mirror Door Room is located. The trash can at the end of the hall sometimes seems to have a mind of its own. One day, many students reported that they watched the lid lift itself up, float down the hall a few feet, then hit the floor and slide the rest of the way down the hall. I have toured the school several times, and have experienced a few unusual sensations, but not much more. It's hard to gain access to some of these areas unless you are a student or faculty member. I hope one day soon to travel to the school with cameras and K2 meters in hand. Until that happens, I believe the large quantities of suspicious paranormal activity reported by students and others would safely allow me to graduate this site to be included among Florida's "Historic Haunts".

34

MANNING THE FORT PARANORMAL STYLE
Fort Castillo de San Marcos, St. Augustine

A Fort by Any Other Name

Man the Fort! This was the cry of the Spanish after an attack on St. Augustine by English privateer Robert Searle in 1668. It became obvious the city needed a stronger fort for its protection, and to answer these concerns Mariana Queen Regent of Spain, approved upgrading the wooden forts to a masonry fortification. The Castillo de San Marcos was built between 1673 and 1695. It took the work of many slaves and soldiers and approximately 23 years to complete. The fort was built of coquina stone, from the quarry on Anastasia Island, which is a very porous stone and can hold or absorb energy (something many unfortunate attackers and pirates learned as their cannonballs embedded in the Fort walls). The fort served the Spanish well for

Early postcard Author's Collection

many years, enduring through many attacks, including a siege attempt by the English during Queen Anne's War in 1702, and bombardment of the structure in 1740 by Governor Oglethorpe of the colony of Georgia. The British came into possession of the Castillo de San Marcos as a provision of the Treaty of Paris in 1763. They renamed it Fort St. Mark. After the end of the American Revolutionary War, the terms of the Treaty of Paris required the British to hand control of the fort back the Spanish in 1783. It would later pass to the U.S. via treaty with Spain. The Americans took over St. Augustine in 1821, renaming the place Fort Marion after Revolutionary war hero Francis Marion.

35

During the Second Seminole War, between 1835 and 1842, the fort served as a military prison for Seminole captives, including the famous Osceola (who was taken while attending a peace conference under a flag of truce). It was also during this war that 20 Indians made a great escape on the east side of the fort. Legend says they starved themselves until they were so thin they could slip through the narrow windows, drop into the moat, and make their escape. This point is under contention, as some historians claim that the guards unlocked the prisoner's cells and turned their backs for the Native Americans to escape (feeling guilty about their capture under false pretenses).

In 1861, when Florida seceded from the Union during the Civil War, and joined the Confederacy; the Confederates took over Fort Marion. This was short lived as the Union took back the Fort in March 1862. After the war in 1870's and 1880's, the fort was again being used to house Indians captives (mostly Plains and Apaches). Several years later in 1898, during the Spanish American War, it was used as a military prison.

The fort has actively served for over 200 years, while under five different flags. During its time in service it was never taken by force. It is said to be the best preserved specimen in the world of the military architecture of its time. In 1924, the fort was designated a National Monument. In 1933, it was transferred to the National Park Service. An act of Congress in 1942 returned it to its previous identity as the Castillo de San Marcos to reflect St. Augustine's Spanish heritage. The park was also listed on the national Register of Historic Places in 1966. It's no wonder after all the years, occupants, and prisoners, the Fort has seen, that there is believed to be so much lingering activity.

The Ghosts at the Fort

As if to reinforce the stories of the Native American prisoners, many people have reported seeing someone or something escaping the narrow windows by night on the east side of the Fort. Very few people seem to dispute the Indians haunting the fort. The company I work for, GhoSt Augustine actually has photos in our possession of the full body apparitions of Native Americans at the fort. The question comes up, are they photos of the Indians who escaped that day or are they ones that suffered and were never able to leave?

The east side of the fort is also where the execution wall was located. In fact, there is an entire wall full of nothing but musket holes, where men were once executed. One evening, when GhoSt Augustine's "Haunted St. Augustine Tour" was touring the outside of the fort I had an experience of my own. That particular night, I decided to tag along with the tour and check on our tour guides. We had just reached the execution wall, when all of the sudden, I felt a tight grip on my right wrist. It got tighter and tighter, almost as if I had shackles on, but only on one wrist. When I looked down there was a red mark all the way around my wrist. When I spoke out, "Stop it!" The tightness went away, but the red mark remained. When the tour group reached an area with better lighting, we looked at my wrist, and commented that it looked like my shackles had been too tight. As the evening progressed, the redness went away, but I couldn't help but wonder who or what caused it. The next day I discovered, after a little more research, that most of the prisoners were in shackles when they were executed.

36

Besides the activity on the east side, there have also been several collective sightings on the north side of the fort. A collective sighting occurs when more than one person witnesses the same phenomenon. These collective sightings have all been reports describing in detail, the apparition of a soldier who appears to still be on guard, walking between the openings at the top of the fort. In addition to the soldier, there are detailed reports also of a woman in a white night gown. She has been seen in this area, as well as others. Some witnesses have even heard the woman's voice, but can never completely make out what she is saying.

As active as these two sides of the Fort are, battle cries are often heard all around the fort grounds. Sounds of musket fire, and even cannon fire have been heard at night when no one is in the fort. These are only a few of the common reports. Over the years, K2 meters on our tours have detected intense activity, and many tour-goers have reported seeing spirits.

The last ghost story that I have frequently heard associated with the fort involves a young officer who is searching the grounds around the moat area. He appears to be looking for something he has lost. He has often been reported, always in uniform, looking down at the ground, and never interacting with anyone.

These stories are only a small sampling of the many reports of paranormal activity detailed by visitors to the Fort. To this day, it is one of the most popular stops on the GhoSt Augustine Paranormal Investigative Tour. In fact, with over 10 years of tours and witnesses behind us, we can say with certainty that the Castillo de San Marcos is a fantastic location full of hundreds of years of history, ghost stories and paranormal phenomenon to match.

GHOST AUGUSTINE TOURS AND THE HAUNTED HEARSES

GhoSt Augustine Hearse Rides, St. Augustine

When you hear the name Historic Haunts, most people think of haunted historic locations, but what if the haunt wasn't a house, a building, or a location? What if it was a car? Not just any car, but a car whose job for years was to carry the bodies of the departed to their final resting place. Considering how many times this type is connected to the deceased, it seems very obvious and believable that a hearse, especially an older one, might be a "Historic Haunt".

Two haunted hearses can be found on GhoSt Augustine's tours. GhoSt Augustine is one of the best ghost tours in St. Augustine (believed by many to be the nation's oldest and most haunted city). Admittedly, I'm a little jaded since I'm the manager, but the tours have consistently been favored by visitors and local publications alike. One of the most popular tours offered by GhoSt Augustine is the original hearse ride. Tour goers are treated to a great tour of some of St. Augustine's most historic locations, conducted in one of two working hearses. These two vehicles have seen several bodies come and go in their tours-of-duty with funeral homes. Now they tour the streets of St. Augustine with the bodies of eager fans of the paranormal. What many of these fans are surprised to learn as they travel the city hearing ghostly tales, is that the hearses themselves are haunted!

"Frankie" | Photo: GhoSt Augustine

"Frankie" the Yankee

Our youngest haunted hearse is nicknamed "Frankie". This vehicle is a 1990 Cadillac that saw extensive duty in New York. There are two main spirits that seem to interact with drivers, visitors and viewers in this vehicle. The first is the spirit of an older man who loved the car dearly, treated it tenderly, and according to research and records, used to drive it when it was an actual working hearse up north. The driver's name was Frank. Frank has manifested himself at times to tourists and tour guides.

38

His voice is sometimes heard in the vehicle and over cell phones, and he has appeared (in whole or in part) as a passenger in the hearse itself. He occasionally makes himself known to travelers on the GhoSt Augustine hearse rides, but appears more often to the tour guides and company employees (perhaps to let us know he is watching us and making sure we are taking care of his car).

Memories of Frank and the Little Stowaway

One of the most memorable appearances Frank has made that I can recall came during an evaluation of a new tour guide. It was a dark and stormy night (as it seems to be in so many good ghost tales). I had gone out with the new tour guide on her tours for the night. It had rained throughout the tour, but we didn't think much of it, sometimes it even makes the tour seem even spookier. On that night, the rain didn't help and we finished up the 9:15 p.m. tour with very little excitement. Unfortunately, the ghosts do not perform on que, and they are sometimes reluctant with new guides. Even so, with over ten years of doing ghost tours under our belts, the spirits in St. Augustine have grown accustomed to us. They seem to make themselves known to us on a more regular basis than some of the more forceful, overcrowded, and intrusive tours in town.

The thunderstorm was growing worse. Radio forecasts at our headquarters confirmed it, citing the possibility of severe lightning, thunder and hail! Having finished all tours for the night, I made the obvious decision to wrap it up and park the hearses in the parking garage (in case the storm was as bad as the weatherman claimed). Our new guide had picked me up at home in Frankie, and so we were heading back to Anastasia Island. The Island is where our main offices are located and where we retire the hearses for the night. Our new guide drove Frankie across the bridge heading toward the island, I followed in her car. The thunderstorm activity had picked up. These types of storms and electrical activity sometimes seem to "charge up" spirits, encouraging paranormal activity. As if to echo this, something unusual appeared and caught my eye as I was following our new guide. We came to a stop and I quickly called the guide on her cell phone. I told her to take a look in the rearview mirror. As she looked up I heard her exclaim, "Holy crap! It's Frank!" We both observed the full image of a man sitting in the middle section behind her, matching the description of Frank. He lingered for a brief time, as if checking up on her, but faded away after she nodded to him and acknowledged his presence.

Frank has made himself known at other times to other people. Many times by way of voices or whispered conversations that are hard to completely make out. One of my earliest encounters with Frank occurred while I was delivering Ghost Tour brochures to different hotels in the hearse. I received a call from my mother, who seldom calls me during the work day. At an upcoming stop I answered, hoping nothing was wrong, and she assured me she was fine, and just wanted to chat. I switched over to my wireless headset and explained to her that I was working and would call her later. She asked me. "Who is that man I hear? He has a very deep voice!" The radio in the hearse hasn't worked for years, and there were no other sounds coming from any devices in the car. I couldn't hear anything, but she kept insisting that she heard a man talking. I have experienced this several times, and being something of a skeptic, my mother and I have changed phones and headsets several times. Maybe Frank likes to hear himself talk, he has "sounded off" in the hearse to other people the same way during other phone conversations on a variety of different cell phones and carriers. However, whether I am off duty or not he seems to enjoy jumping in on mine (especially with my mom).

Besides Frank the sounds of another spirit is sometimes encountered in this hearse. This spirit is much younger and is referred to by GhoSt Augustine as "Emily". Emily was the name of an 11 year old girl who died suddenly, and whose coffin had been transported in Frankie to the cemetery. The sounds of Emily's laughter are often heard in the hearse during tours. She is very playful, loves to pull tour-goer's pony tails, and make the K2 meters go off between stops (especially when kids are holding the meters). Many have speculated that she is unaware she has passed and is looking for attention and playmates.

Ms. Tariqa | Photo: GhoSt Augustine

The Fabulous Ms. Tariqa

The second hearse GhoSt Augustine uses for our tours has been nicknamed "Ms. Tariqa" or just Tariqa. She is the largest of our hearses, and has something of a magnetic personality that seems to draw the most attention from tour guides and visitors. As a 1974 model, she is our "cagey veteran". Temperamental sometimes, she has her own ways of getting noticed. Her favorite is "hide and seek". Items carried by tour guides and tourists inside Tariqa will sometimes vanish, only to show up later, most frequently reappearing in the center of the back area (where the coffins used to go). Purses, umbrellas, and other items have all been known to play a part in the game. In many cases, items in the front seat disappear, only to show up later in the center of the back.

One of my favorite stories involving Tariqa though, occurred several years ago. Jonas Brehammer, the owner of GhoSt Augustine, had gone to pick Tariqa up from the repair shop where she was undergoing routine maintenance. He noticed sand in the hearse, and decided to climb in and sweep it out while he waited for the repairman to total the bill. Jonas paid the bill, went to reach for his keys and realized they were gone. Unfazed, he figured that they must have fallen out of his pocket while he was cleaning. He began looking throughout the hearse for the keys. After some extensive searching, he became a bit more concerned. Tariqa was scheduled for a tour in a couple of hours and he seemed to be unable to locate the keys. He enlisted the assistance of the shops repairmen, and together they spent quite a while tearing the car apart in an unsuccessful effort to find the keys. By now, very concerned, Jonas called the store and was relieved to find out that the tour group scheduled that night was small enough to squeeze into the other hearse "Frankie". Finally giving up, he left Tariqa there. Early the next morning, one of the mechanics called and told Jonas they had found the keys! He asked them where they found them. The repairman, sounding completely surprised and baffled replied "Right in the back of the hearse, right out in the open, in the middle, where the coffins used to go!" Apparently Tariqa didn't want to work that night.

Tariqa and Her Favorites

Tariqa seems to have favorites, becoming more active with certain tour guides and drivers. One of Tariqa's favorites is Tina Verduzco. One night I was out with Tina, while she did her "dress rehearsal" on her way to becoming a full-fledged tour guide. I was excited to do a dress rehearsal with Tina because I knew she was already a unique, and very expressive, artist and person, and I thought she would be a great tour guide and story teller. She picked me up in Ms. Tariqa and began her introduction as all our tour guides do, by putting their own personal flair on things (making each tour and tour guide unique). As we turned down St. George Street, Tina mentioned to me that her husband Paul had passed a few years ago. I was very sorry to hear this. Tina is a very spiritual person, and she went on to tell me that she often felt Paul's spirit comforting and reassuring her. This was especially true when she was alone or working late by herself. I could tell by her voice that Tina was nervous. It was at about that time that Tina and I felt a sudden chill and presence occurring right between us and sending goose bumps up the length of our arms. I made the comment that I thought Paul was along for the ride. She commented that she was going to need his help getting through it. After our little "incident" Tina seemed much more self-assured and confident. She passed the dress rehearsal with flying colors and has gone on to be one of our most popular tour guides. She and her tour-goers have experienced Paul in the hearse in many ways since then. But my favorite, needless to say, was when Tina had a little help passing her dress rehearsal from her "spirited" husband.

Besides Paul, and the mischievous "hide and seek", Tariqa likes to make herself known more directly. Sometimes by making sure she is on everyone's mind and the center of conversation. It was during a very special night a short time ago, that Tariqa decided to call in others to join in on the discussion. Three of GhoSt Augustine's tour guides and I were standing around her and discussing the tours going out that evening. We were also comparing notes for a time, about the paranormal events that had been taking place lately on the tours, and of course, the fabulous Ms. Tariqa! That evening, our tour guide Brandy Klopp was to be Tariqa's driver. Brandy (another of Tariqa's favorites), had left her personal belongings in the front seat of Tariqa, and her cell phone face up beside them. We could all see this through the front and side windows of the parked hearse. We finished our conversation, and nailed down the route and plan for the night after about 20 minutes. We were about to go our separate ways when we were surprised to hear Brandy's phone ringing. It was Tina Verduzco calling. We could all hear Tina's voice from the phone as she began with "Sorry I missed your calls, what's up?" Brandy was a little confused and asked Tina what the heck she was talking about. Tina replied, "You called me three times in the last 20 minutes!" Brandy told Tina that she hadn't made any calls, she had been standing around talking with me and the other tour guides the whole time, and that her phone had been in the car the entire time. We all started laughing as we realized Tariqa must have called, wanting Tina to get in on the conversation! Ms. Tariqa has "ghost dialed" several people from several different phones since then.

Parting Thoughts

Tariqa and Frankie are just another reason why my job is so interesting. Weird things tend to happen, not just on tours, but in the hearses as well. In fact, these types of things have become almost second nature to us. If you visit St. Augustine, make sure you check out one of GhoSt Augustine's tours. If you are a little creeped out by riding in a real hearse, then try out the Haunted Pub Tour where you will encounter Spirits with Spirits. If you're more into the scientific side of the paranormal, join the Haunted St. Augustine tour. These are some of our most popular tours, although GhoSt Augustine features several other ghost tours as well. In addition, we have a fantastic selection of ghost hunting equipment available, which we supply to those interested in the paranormal, amateur ghost hunters, and popular televised ghost hunters alike. Don't just take my word for it though, as I said before, I might be a little biased. Come check it out for yourself. If you do, maybe you can say hello to Tariqa and Frankie.

THE WHITE NUN
Mission of Nombre De Dios, St. Augustine

It's "Murphy's Law" that seems to come into play sometimes with many paranormal experiences. For paranormal investigators and enthusiasts, this means that the best evidence will present itself when you are ill-prepared to gather it. Often times the best activity begins when the cameras and recorders are off, when there are few witnesses left or worse yet, when you are doing normal day-to-day tasks and have no means to capture it! This was the case for me one day at the Mission of Nombre De Dios.

The Unlucky Chapel

In 1728, the Chapel of Our Lady of La Leche, the first chapel built of stone, stood in all its glory in St. Augustine. British Colonel, John Palmer, member of Commons House of Assembly in SC, attempted to subdue St. Augustine. The Spanish fired upon the chapel from the Castillo de San Marcos to prevent Palmer from using the building. This shelling damaged it extensively

Mission of Nombre De Dios | Photo: Author

Bishop Augustin Verot (the 1st Bishop of the Diocese of St. Augustine) built another chapel in 1875. Shortly after it was built, it was severely damaged by a hurricane. The Chapel remained in this storm damaged, state of disrepair, until the intervention of Bishop Michael Curley. Curley would later go on to become Arch Bishop of Baltimore, but not before he restored the Chapel to the condition it remains in to this day. The Chapel had a cemetery that surrounded it known as the Mission of Nombre De Dios. It was established in 1884, shortly before the Tolomato and Huguenot cemeteries were closed in town. This became the new cemetery for the Catholics until San Lorenzo Cemetery opened in 1890.

My Experiences with the Haunted Chapel & the Prayers of the White Nun

Many people are drawn to the large cross (reportedly the biggest in the world) and the grounds of the Mission. I am one of them. The grounds of the Mission are one of my favorite places to take a walk in the evening. It is a beautiful place to enjoy peace, quiet, and solitude away from the busy Spanish City (something I think the nuns and bishops must have known as well). As I was walking through the cemetery one evening, I found that for some reason the door on the Chapel caught my eye. It looked like they had either installed a new door or had stained the old one. For some reason, I

43

was drawn to it! I touched the door to see if the stain was still wet and it felt like it had been there for years, but something looked different. I had never noticed a slight gap between the two doors and decided to peek inside. I could see a lit candle on the mantel, which I thought was rather strange since it was after hours and everything was locked up tight. Why would they leave a candle lit all night? As I was gazing at the candle, a woman in a white habit walked over in front of the altar, and knelt down. She was totally transparent, and I could tell without a doubt she was a nun. She began praying. I stood there totally amazed, looking at her, not believing what I was seeing and aggravated at my lack of equipment.

Transfixed, I continued watching her with her head bowed and hands clasped until I heard the sounds of another woman walking around the trail, and coming towards the chapel. Unfortunately, just as I heard the noises, so too did the spirit in the chapel. She rose up, crossed herself, and turned to leave vanishing as she did so! I just stood there for a second, not really believing what I saw. The other walker passed me as I reflected on what I'd seen. The nun was what we call an intelligent haunt, not residual. She actually heard the other walker coming and reacted by leaving. Apparently she hadn't noticed me or didn't mind me being there. I have walked the Mission grounds several times since that fateful night, alone and with others, but have yet to see the white nun again. Whether she was seeking solitude or salvation, I pray someday I experience her again.

44

THE MISFORTUNE MUSEUM
Tragedy in the U.S History Museum, St. Augustine

Fighting Hard for Misfortune

Many people have a curious interest in the grisly details of tragic events. It is the stuff of sensational journalism and dramatic television. L.H. Buddy Hough, a resident of St. Augustine, was aware of the public's fixation with tragedies and thought it would be a fantastic idea for a museum attraction. In 1963, after Kennedy's assassination, he became inspired to open just such a museum. He began to acquire many morbid items related to tragic U.S. events. Buddy also secured permits and began turning the house at 7 Williams Street, that he and his wife occupied, into his dream museum.

Ironically, St. Augustine, a town full of museums, and the home of noteworthy oddities at Ripley's, disapproved of Buddy's vision and thought his odd collection was a little too much! The town's city commissioners began actively working to shut the museum down. In 1965 Hough's fight with the city to open his museum went all the way to the Florida Supreme Court, and three years later he won. He was finally able to open his Tragedy in the U.S. History Museum. However, even after he was given permission to open Buddy discovered he still had to fight for recognition and with the city to keep it open.

The Supreme Court loss left as bad of a taste in the city commissioner's mouths as the tragic items in the museum's collection. Buddy discovered that curious callers to the city's Chamber of Commerce were repeatedly and forcefully told the museum had closed! Local tourist's trams drove by quickly, never stopping and seldom mentioning the museum. Mr. Hough's museum was even tragically omitted from most of St. Augustine's various tourist brochures. Despite all the efforts of the City to work against him, Buddy continued to fight. He fought this battle all the way up to the time of his death in 1996. After his death, his widow, disheartened, eventually gave up the fight. On April 4th, 1998 she auctioned everything off and sold the building. Buddy's dream was now more tragic history.

Tragic Souvenirs

The Tragedy in the U.S. History Museum boasted quite a collection of tragic momentos. Many noted paranormal experts believe tragic items can sometimes carry energies themselves. In fact, many visitors to the museum reported odd occurrences in the vicinity of these tragic artifacts. Among the odd and possibly morbid items in the museum's collection were:

- A real Egyptian Mummy
- Some of the Living room furniture from the room where Lee Harvey Oswald took the shot that killed President Kennedy
- Two real human skeletons in an 18th century Spanish jail cell
- A mockup of the famous cow that started the great Chicago Fire, October 8th, 1871 (Including overturned bucket and lantern)

The museum proudly displayed the car that was used in the classic movie Bonnie and Clyde (starring Warren Beatty and Faye Dunaway). This particular piece was

45

meant to illustrate the tragic end that one of this country's most famous bank robbers suffered. The original death car held 137 bullet holes and the museum depicted this with photos from the original crime scene.

Buddy was extremely interested in the Kennedy assassination and the Museum supposedly had the original hearse that carried John F. Kennedy's body, the same hearse that was rumored to have carried Lee Harvey Oswald's body as well. In addition, the museum allegedly contained the white Lincoln Continental that President Kennedy was actually shot in. Museum patrons reported that anyone trying to photograph the car would have camera malfunctions, or that strange anomalies would appear in the photos. According to these reports no one was successfully able to capture a photo of the Continental.

Researching the Museum's Tragic End

The former museum site as it looks today

Photo: Author

In my research, I hadn't come across any reports of people seeing apparitions at the museum, but I did hear some interesting stories and experienced some interesting things myself. When I first moved to St. Augustine I would take walks in the evenings and explore the neighborhoods. I walked by this building so many times and never knew what it housed at one point in the past. There is a very heavy feeling in this location, especially in and around the building where the museum once stood. It always felt so heavy to me as if someone was pushing down on me but I could never explain why. Sometimes, I would catch myself just staring at the building wondering what was there, what had been there, or who was still there. I never did see anything, but that feeling that a presence was there, always returned when I got close. At times it felt like I was feeling the sadness and fear attached to someone else's pain. There is the possibility that these lingering sounds or feelings coming from the area where the museum once stood, are caused by energy from all the tragic items that used to be housed in the building. To this day these feelings are described by many on this spot.

Investigating this "Historic Haunt" was a little more difficult since it no longer exists, but once I learned a little more about Mr. Hough's museum, I tried to find eyewitnesses or someone who might provide more insight into the strange feelings I was sensing. Interesting enough, I actually found and interviewed a retired couple who lived just a few doors down from the museum while it was open, and for a few years after it closed. They described hearing strange noises from the museum at night when no one was around, even after the contents of the museum had been sold off. They could clearly make out the sounds of someone in pain or distress. They even mentioned the heavy feeling around the area where the museum had been located. They said it was like a heavy wall, that you could feel, but when you stepped a few feet away, everything felt fine.

Perhaps the building is now haunted by the deceased Mr. Hough. Maybe he doesn't know that his battle with the city was lost or that he has passed on. Maybe the biggest tragedy of all is that we may never know. The story of this Historic Haunt reads like a tragedy itself, but hopefully one that won't fade like yesterday's headlines.

SOMETHING ABOUT A MAN IN UNIFORM
Old Florida Naval Academy, St. Augustine

A Rich Naval History

The former Naval Academy

Photo: Author

A strong naval presence has always been found in St. Augustine. During World War II, the U.S. Navy even maintained a state naval academy in the city. The Florida Naval Academy was located near the Fountain of Youth in St. Augustine. Many naval officers were trained here, and in fact new barracks for the Florida Naval Academy were built in 1942. The academy weathered many storms during the heights of World War II and a literal one in 1944. After World War II ended and the navy restructured, the base was closed, The recently built barracks were converted to an apartment building. This was where I lived when I first moved to St. Augustine.

Peacocks and Indians

It is scary enough living right next door to the Fountain of Youth, especially at night. The old tree-lined Magnolia Street, draped as it is, with creepy Spanish moss, seems to be peering at you and definitely gives you an uneasy feeling. Even creepier (until I got used to them) are the peacocks that reside at the Fountain of Youth Park. When they start making their calls at night, they almost sound like a woman in distress. Besides the peacocks, there is documented historical fact that the Timucua Indian Burial grounds have been found inside the park's walls. Together these elements are unnerving enough, but the entire area seems to give many people (myself included) an intensely haunted and uneasy feeling.

The Ghostly Serviceman

I never considered the idea of my apartment building being haunted until one night when I couldn't sleep. I got up and decided I would watch a little television until I got sleepy enough to go back to bed. I went over to the window trying to catch a glimpse of the full moon. This night the light of the full moon revealed a young man in some sort of uniform walking around the back courtyard looking towards the ground. He appeared to be looking for something. As i stared more intently I noticed he wasn't an ordinary man. Under closer scrutiny I realized he was transparent! I watched him for about 60 seconds. He was oblivious to my staring. He just kept looking for whatever he had lost, until he ultimately disappeared.

I caught myself looking out the windows at the back courtyard for the next several nights, hoping he might come back. I had just about given up when the next full moon came. There was the soldier, walking the same path looking down at the ground still searching. He appeared and disappeared just as before. After that I decided, like the soldier, to search for more details. Unfortunately, my research into the soldier's identity proved unsuccessful. However, after discussion with other tenants in the complex I discovered I wasn't the only one who had spotted the soldier's ghost. There were many longtime residents who speculated that the soldier might be someone who lost his life during the great storm of 1944, but no one was sure. What is known is that he is still sometimes seen by tenants on a full moon. I would soon discover that he wasn't the only ghost in the apartment complex.

An Indian Returns?

It wasn't long after my discovery of the ghost soldier and my move in day that I had my next paranormal experience. I hadn't detected anything in my apartment, but had just finished wading through moving boxes. After several days I was starting to finally feel settled in. The workday had ended and I was trying to hurry home and beat a terrible storm that was heading my way. I made it through the door just as the skies opened up. I walked into my apartment and felt immensely uneasy!! My apartment had never felt creepy like this before. I closed the door behind me and walked into my bedroom to unload everything I had brought up from the car. Suddenly, I had the feeling that I was definitely not alone! I started turning on all the lights in the apartment to try and comfort myself, but I began feeling more and more uneasy. I didn't really want to be there alone. Having investigated many paranormal sites, I don't get spooked easily, but this time, I had to admit, I was just a little freaked out.

You could feel the barometric pressure drop, the air got heavier and heavier, and the temperature dropped drastically. I spoke up in the empty apartment and saying," Who is here? Show yourself? "As I left the bedroom heading to another part of the apartment, I noticed a very dark shadowy figure in the doorway to the bathroom. He was at least 6 foot 4 inches tall, had very broad shoulders, and was extremely dark with no major identifiable characteristics. I shouted out, "I don't know who you are, but in the name of God get out of my house!" No sooner had I finished my sentence, than the figure was gone.

As soon as I calmed down, and the room began to feel normal again, the researcher in me took hold. Many paranormal experts believe that electrical storms create enough energy for spirits to feed off of and materialize. The storm that night certainly fit the bill and could explain the figure's sudden appearance. I dug a little deeper over the next few days, trying to find out who the figure could have been. Locals had told me that the building was built on Indian burial grounds. I didn't find any documented proof of that, but the Timucua Indians were known to be well over 6 feet tall, and they did live in the area. In fact, a known Indian burial ground was found right next door by archeologists in 1934, at the Fountain of Youth Park. The thought that the burial grounds might have extended under the apartment complex was not that far-fetched. This wouldn't be the first time St. Augustine had built a structure upon graves (see A1A Aleworks). Unfortunately, I was unable to come up with any more suggestions to my visitor's identity. I never saw him again, even on stormy nights. Some in the paranormal field believe you can usher a spirit out by declaring the place to be yours and demanding they leave. If this is true, perhaps my exclamation that dark stormy night was enough to chase him away, or perhaps he found an apartment he liked better!

THE KEEPER'S GHOST
St. Augustine Lighthouse

St. Augustine Lighthouse

Photo: Author

St. Augustine's Light in the Darkness

Crashing into rocks was always a hazard for early sea-farers. In the late 1500's a Spanish watchtower was built, to look for boats among other things and was the predecessor of the current lighthouse. Florida's first American lighthouse was built in 1824, and was in St. Augustine. In 1870, the tower was threatened by erosion and the shoreline was slowly washing away. Construction soon began on the present lighthouse on a spot more protected from erosion. The tower that stands today was first lit on October 15th, 1874. In 1880, the old light fell into the sea during a horrific storm. The current light house is the oldest surviving brick structure in St. Augustine. A keeper's house was later built in 1876, as the living quarters for the light keepers and their families. The light keeper's house, interestingly enough has a basement, and this beautiful brick home is built on a hill; locals jokingly call it Mount Anastasia. The hill of course provides just enough height above sea level to allow for the full basement.

The St. Augustine Lighthouse's beautiful tower rises 165 feet above sea level, and consists of 219 steps to the top. The U.S. Coast Guard turned the light house and grounds over to the St. Augustine Lighthouse Museum, Inc. in 2002. This was the pilot program for the National Historic Lighthouse Preservation Act. There is no way of knowing, without this act, what might have happened to this historic landmark and many others like it.

Ghosts of Keepers Past?

The lighthouse and grounds have been notorious for paranormal activity for a very long time. However, it gained national notoriety when featured on a popular televised ghost investigation series in 2006. Like many of the reports by eyewitnesses, investigators heard a disembodied voice, and saw a figure leaning over the railing looking at them. The figure reappeared higher and higher in the tower, but never set off their motion detectors (although their cameras did record his presence).

The Lightkeeper's house

Photo: Author

My first paranormal experience was several years ago while inside the Keeper's House. I was playing tourist and was getting tired of following the

49

crowd, so I ventured off on my own to go explore the basement. It was almost as if I was being drawn to the basement for some reason. As I descended down the narrow spiral staircase, the air seemed to change gradually. It seemed to get heavier and heavier, keeping pace with me the farther down the staircase I walked. The temperature also felt as if it was dropping with each step I took (and more than you would think from going deep underground). I looked past the water cisterns, and down the short narrow hallway, as I reached the foot of the stairs. To my surprise, I saw a man dressed in a blue uniform and hat (almost like a Naval officer or sea captain would wear).He was fairly tall, and had a partial beard. He appeared to be in his mid to late 50's. He walked from the left to the right in the room at the end of the hall.

My first thought, was that I had happened upon an actor interpreting someone from the lighthouse's past. So I went down the hallway to see who he was, and what story he was interpreting. I continued down the short hallway to the room at the end, fully expecting to see a man standing in the little room. The closer I got to the room, the more the air temperature seemed to drop. The difference became drastic and the air got even heavier! This was St. Augustine, in the middle of June; it doesn't get this cold in a building unless the air conditioner is set on arctic! As I finally reached the room, I turned the corner in the same direction where I had seen the bearded man go and there was no one there! He was nowhere to be found. There were no doors to go through, and no place else he could have disappeared to, this was a dead end. Could this possibly have been one of the past light keepers? This was the first and only time I have seen an apparition at the lighthouse but not my only paranormal experience.

In autumn of 2010, I was interviewed as part of the cable channel show entitled Most Terrifying Places in America. They asked me to describe on camera my experience of seeing the sea captain's apparition in the basement of the keeper's house. While I was waiting for the others being interviewed to finish up, I began to smell the distinct smell of sweet pipe smoke. It was actually a very pleasant smell. There was no one to be found anywhere other than the film crew, and the other people being interviewed. No one on site was smoking. Captain Rasmusson, a former light keeper (who coincidentally matched my description of the bearded sea captain) was known to be a pipe smoker. Many visitors claim to have experienced the overwhelming smell of sweet tobacco suddenly appearing out of thin air. Coincidentally, the person being interviewed at the exact moment I first experienced the pipe smoke, was actually talking about the captain and the smoke on camera. Maybe he was just stopping by to see who was talking about him, and what was being said?!

This is only one of many stories involving the lighthouse. Many people have experienced other paranormal activity, and I have personally seen the K2 meters become very active while exploring the site with other visitors. If you want to shed more light on the St. Augustine lighthouse, her stories and resident spirits, I recommend you take GhoSt Augustine's Hearse Ride and encounter these things for yourself.

50

THE LAWMAN'S GHOST
Old St. Johns County Jail

Old St. John's County Jail | Photo: Author

Story of a Jail

It was pretty much Henry Flagler's St. Augustine in the late 1800s. When the railroad magnate had The Hotel Ponce De Leon built in 1887, he was very unhappy about the St. Johns County Jail located just across the street. Flagler was concerned that the jail would scare potential guests away from his luxurious new hotel. So, Henry donated $10,000 to the county to have a new jail built, (far enough outside of town so that it wouldn't affect his business).

The Old St. Johns County Jail was constructed in 1891 by the Pauly Jail Building & Manufacturing Company. They would later go on to build the infamous Alcatraz in 1934. The jail housed as many as 72 prisoners at a time from 1891 to 1953. It featured men and women's cells, maximum security cells, and a death row cell. General population was housed upstairs while the maximum security, women's cells, and death row cell were all located downstairs along with the kitchen. Only 8 hangings were conducted in the sixty plus years this building served as the county jail. The inmates endured some pretty intense conditions with open windows and only bars protecting them from the weather. None of the cells had indoor plumbing. Prisoners needing to relieve themselves would use a bucket and in the mid-summer Florida heat, it made living with the smell in the cells almost unbearable. Unlike the prisoners, Sheriff Joe Perry, a very popular local sheriff, maintained living quarters that were actually attached to the prison, but he and his family lived in luxury.

Greetings from the Gallows

When I lived in St. Augustine I lived literally two blocks behind the old jail. I would often take walks at night when the temperature cooled itself, and prowl around some

51

of the old buildings in town. More often than not, I would walk around the jail. Usually by that time of night all the businesses were closed, people were in bed, and all the tourists were back in their hotel rooms exhausted from a long day of exploring.

One night I was walking back from the Mission and I figured I would take the road that runs right behind the jail. I had just walked past the jail, when all of a sudden I was startled by a loud bang! When I looked up the gallows had dropped. I looked around, but saw no one else. At times like these I wish I had a fellow witness and my equipment. When I looked up at the staircase situated on the backside of the building, I saw a rather large man. The man stood well over 6 feet tall with broad shoulders, and was wearing a hat. He was looking at the gallows. When he noticed me, he nodded his head and then vanished!

Could this have been the ghost of Sheriff Perry? Many paranormal reports would suggest that people seem to think he is still there. I did a little research after my unexpected experience, and found a picture of the late Joe Perry. The photo bore a strong resemblance to the man that I saw. Records indicated that the Sheriff was around 6 feet 4 inches tall, and always wore a hat. I have walked past the old jail several times since that night. Many times I have heard noises and sounds, but I haven't yet had the pleasure of another friendly nod from this mysterious, tall man. The Old Jail remains a fascinating tourist spot, a stop for local ghost tours, and a "Historic Haunt" that fans of the paranormal should definitely investigate. If you go, be sure to tip your hat to the sheriff if you see him.

THE SERIAL KILLER
AND THE ELECTRIC CHAIR
Old Sparky, Florida's Electric Chair, Raiford

A Shocking History

Death by electrocution has been a highly debated topic for years, especially in Florida. When the title Historic Haunts comes to mind, most people wouldn't think of a haunted location being an electric chair. Not just any electric chair though, Sparky is Florida's old electric chair at Raiford. It is definitely a historic piece of Florida's past. Although several other states have electric chairs nicknamed "sparky" Florida's electric chair is unique in the reported cases of the paranormal. Sparky was Florida's sole means of execution from 1924 to 2000, but no one has been electrocuted since 1999 in this historic chair.

As of this printing, the electric chair is no longer the main means of execution in Florida, but death row prisoners can request this means of execution if they prefer. By the 1990's the chair had become known for frequent malfunctions. On May 4th, 1990, Jesse Tafero was executed after being found guilty for killing two Florida Highway Patrol Officers. During his execution six inch flames shot from his head. On March 25th, 1997, Pedro Medina was executed for brutally killing a woman. During his final moments, 12 inch flames shot from his head during the execution. Controversy spread even more after the July 8th, 1999 execution of Allen Lee Davis. Davis, who was sent to the electric chair for a number of murders he committed, experienced Sparky's malfunctions too. During his execution, his white shirt turned blood red when he developed a profuse nose bleed during the final moments before his death. It was believed that this was most likely caused by the head strap not fitting him properly. This incident made the debate over the electric chair, and whether it was a humane means of execution, an even more heated topic than it had become from the last two executions.

Investigators believed the malfunctions could have been due to a partial upgrade several years earlier. The chair portion was replaced, but the electrical components were not updated.

In addition, to insure proper contact between the inmates head and the electrodes during execution, a saline soaked sponge was stuffed between the two. Tafero's execution, it was believed had been carried out incorrectly, because the sponges that were used caught fire. The dry sponges and the fact that they are synthetic are two explanations, thought to be contributing factors to what caused the flames during his execution.

During Medina's execution the sponges were once again not soaked properly which, like Tafero, caused the flames during his death. So, Sparky's history has been marred by improper maintenance to the chair and improper care taken during the setup of the execution.

53

The Current Ghost

The ghost story that came up frequently and was related to Sparky had nothing to do with the three executions that suffered malfunctions. Although it is likely that the death row killers may haunt the chair anyway. In an effort to confirm the startling reports I uncovered, I spoke with a widow whose deceased husband used to work in the prison, while Sparky was in use. Her husband had told her that several people reported seeing the ghost of Ted Bundy sitting in the chair. His spirit seemed comfortable, as if he were sitting reposed in his recliner at home, relaxing after a long day. The prison guard told his wife that several guards have experienced identical activity. When anyone saw Bundy's spirit in the chair he wasn't strapped down, he was just sitting there with a grin on his face as if he were up to something, yet again. If anyone tried to approach him or the chair he would instantly vanish before their eyes.

Reports also indicate that he would occasionally speak to the guards; making comments like, "Well, I beat you, didn't I?" Was this Bundy's way of saying he might be dead, but he isn't gone yet?

The widow went on to tell me that her husband and all the other guards were warned by the warden not to discuss this. They were told that if they spoke of the appearance of Bundy's ghost, or his paranormal interaction to anyone, they would be fired. The warden's threat may have been unnecessary though as the sight of a dead serial killer staring at them was more than enough to scare a few guards into quitting and others into keeping silent. Sparky is no longer used on a regular basis for Florida executions, although prisoners can make a request to face this form of death. The shocking reports of the paranormal return of one of the country's most notorious serial killers are disturbing to say the least. With the intense debate over execution in the state of Florida, it may be easy to understand why authorities have worked to contain these reports. Still, the chair remains an ominous, but fascinating piece of Florida's haunted history.

THE HISTORIC INN AND THE GHOSTLY BLAZE

Ritz Historic Inn, Ocala

Ritz Historic Inn

Photo: Author

A Partying Place

In 1925, Bert Acker and Ocala Judge Simeon Sistrunk had a vision. They wanted to build a beautiful apartment building to service tenants in Ocala. Construction began on what is now known as the Ritz Historic Inn in 1925. It was finished in 1926, and consisted of 16 apartments. Upon completion, the building was named the Ritz Acker Apartments. The elegance and opulence of these apartments soon drew several high profile and well-to-do tenants. During the heady days of the prohibition era, this was the place to be in Ocala. With underground suppliers, and rich residents living in the apartments, grand parties were thrown in the large meeting halls built for the residents and their guests to use.

It was during one of these well-attended, rich drinking galas that a horrific fire broke out in the building. People were screaming in fear for their lives. Trying to desperately escape the building, at least one woman was killed (along with her two dogs) in the fire because she became trapped in her room. No one knows what caused the fire, but suspicions centered around the illegal alcohol trade.

In 1941, three of the apartments were split to make 6. Several other changes were made as well to this beautiful Mediterranean-style apartment building, due to the high demand for housing in the area during World War II. The building didn't become a hotel until the 1980's and she was a hit as her lavish appearance drew several guests and fans. The Inn is now on the National Register of Historic Places, and is going through yet another renovation.

A Burning Question of Ghosts

I uncovered several reports regarding paranormal activity at the old apartments. To this day the sounds of screams are sometimes reported to be heard coming from behind these walls, especially from the portion of the building where the fire occurred. Eyewitnesses described hearing sounds that made them feel as if people are still

55

trapped in there trying to escape the blaze. Other reports include elements of people smelling smoke, and the sounds of people running down the halls towards the exit doors and down the stairwell. This seems to be a residual haunt, since there are no reports of a specific presence interacting with anyone. A residual or "cinematic haunting" occurs when an event just replays itself over and over with no interaction with the viewers. Often times a traumatic event can be trapped inside a location, like a projector playing the same movie over and over. In many cases a contributing factor to these residual haunts is thought by many to be quartz, coquina, and limestone. These materials seem to absorb spiritual energy, and residual haunts have been known to be found in areas like this with high concentrations.

While visiting the hotel researching the book, I discovered it was going through major renovations to restore the old girl to her glory years. I was photographing the building and it was a very hot and muggy day, well into the 90's. A friend, who was with me, to my right, suddenly experienced a cold chill and said, "Look! I'm covered in goose bumps!" I touched his arm and discovered it was a good 10 degrees cooler than the air temperature. As I touched his arm, I too felt the unnatural chill. We both looked at each other, unsure of the cause. I decided to ask if there was anyone there with us, in the same manner that many paranormal investigators do. As soon as I did, my K2 EMF Meter spiked! Just as the meter spiked we both smelled an overwhelming burst of choking smoke surrounding us. We both felt as though the energy of the frantic fire victims and their experience was surrounding us. No sooner did we acknowledge it verbally than it disappeared. We tried to entice the sensations to return on that spot and in other areas around the building, but could not repeat it or get the K2 meter to go off that way again. There seems to be a lot of residual energy still lingering on site. Perhaps the current renovations are stirring things up a bit? During my visit, I tried speaking with the constructions workers. As soon as I brought it up they became visibly pale and nervously refused to discuss it.

I will definitely be going back after the renovations to see if the activity continues. I hope that when the restoration is done this "Historic Haunt" will once again shine as she did so long ago.

SUPERNATURAL NEIGHBORS
Seven Sisters Bed & Breakfast, Ocala

Uninvited Guests

Sometimes your reputation is all you have. In the case of the Seven Sisters Bed and Breakfast, this is especially true since the place no longer exists. Despite renovations and many efforts to remain in business, this famed bed and breakfast has closed its doors. While they were open, these two amazing and neighboring historic houses had gained a reputation for being haunted and apparently had some great paranormal stories to tell.

Seven Sisters Bed & Breakfast | Photo: Author

The Pink House

First there was the "pink house", which was known as the "good house". Referred to as "The Scot House" in the Historical Records, and built in 1888, it was the older of the two homes. During its heyday, it had a brighter appearance and happier feeling than its neighbor. A fact that seems to be reflected even in the stories of the paranormal attached to the house.

There is a young boy who is believed to still haunt these halls. Playful and curious, he enjoys getting into people's personal things. Is he enticing people to play or looking for someone to play with? At times giggling can be heard paired with the sounds of running in the upstairs hallway. Many have suggested the spirit is playing hide and seek darting in and out of the rooms. According to many witnesses he also likes to sneak up behind someone to get them to turn around, and when they do, there is of course no one there.

Another ghostly resident of the pink house is an older gentleman who seems to be a residual haunt since he doesn't interact with anyone. He has been seen repeatedly walking down the hallway and into the same room, all the while, oblivious to anyone or anything around him.

It's not just men that haunt the pink house, however, there is also the mysteriously dressed up woman. Formally dressed or "dressed to the nines" as they would say during those days; she is seen walking through walls that were once believed to have been doorways while she was a guest. While the lady has been reported more often walking through old areas of the house, unlike the older gentleman, she does interact with people.

57

The Pink House's Other Ghostly Caretakers

While the Seven Sisters was an operational Bed and Breakfast, candles were typically lit at night in the guest's rooms and the entry way to provide an old time ambiance. Many people have witnessed the full-blown body apparition of a woman approaching the candles and blowing them out, before leaving the room or disappearing. The front door was often locked when someone entered the house and didn't lock it behind them. Maybe the former owners were trying to keep an eye on the house and keep the guests safe and sound. The ghost had also reportedly been known to lock the door when people left the house. So guests were instructed to remember to take their key with them, even if they only left to go out and get a newspaper. The lady of the house (who had been experienced numerous times and in many different ways) always had a tendency to tidy up after people. Guests had sometimes taken a book from the reading room and left it somewhere else in the house, only to find it returned to its rightful place. She has even been known to unpack guests travel bags and put things in the dresser or the closet.

The spirits in the pink house seem to be very helpful and are at peace caring for their old home. According to several witness reports, they are just doing everyday routines intended to keep the house and everyone in it safe and sound. So much so in fact, that one guest even had an experience on the staircase. As she was descending the staircase she lost her footing and would have tripped, tumbling down the stair. She felt something grab the back of her shirt to help her keep her balance. Whoever or whatever it was pulled her backwards, correcting her position so she would not fall down the stairs.

The Purple House

If the pink house was known for having a positive influence on the guests, the purple house on the other hand was a totally different story. It was built in 1892, and had earned a reputation as the bad or unfriendly house. There were several paranormal reports describing intense and frightening arguments heard throughout the house. Guests reported that the atmosphere in the house just before the strange arguments are overheard turned very heavy and dark. Most witnesses gave details which made it appear that a confrontation was taking place, the conversation were impossible to fully make out. In most of these cases though, one of the speakers, a male spirit, seemed to become enraged.

A Bad Influence

Former guests of the popular bed and breakfast made some startling reports of direct interaction with the building's spirits or spooks in a decidedly negative way. People have frequently reported being pushed up or down the steps by unseen hands on their backs and shoulders. Many of these guests described feeling a male presence accompanied by a heavy and dark sensation. These paranormal encounters were often so violent or confrontational, that guests tried to check out early or to move over into the pink house, because they didn't want to stay in the purple house anymore. While researching the occurrences in the purple house, I came across no specific tragedies in the home or noted male guests. However, there was some evidence to suggest that the purple house is actually built above Indian graves, and this could be what is causing the negative energy in the house.

The Sisters Close Up Shop

Unfortunately, with the decline in the economy, Seven Sisters underwent foreclosure and both houses were put up for auction together. The purple house now sits vacant and is still purple. The pink house has been repainted a new shade of beige and is a lawyer's office. I find it interesting that the new owners put the office in the reportedly friendlier houses. Maybe they had experiences of their own in there?

The Seven Sisters paranormal activity had garnered it quite a reputation, and was one of the main areas I came to Ocala to research for my book. I was disappointed to learn these old buildings had been sold and the bed and breakfast was gone. Still, in an effort to be thorough, I parked my car and walked around investigating. I thought the new owners could shed some light on the buildings, their history and stories. I knocked, and was surprised to see a rather annoyed looking gentleman darting his head in the window long enough to respond, "IT'S NOT HAUNTED!" I thought to myself I didn't ask that. It was interesting that they denied something they hadn't even been asked about.

Whether the current residents of the pink house have experienced paranormal activity or not the previous owners of the house had. They were so sure of it, in fact, that they invited a noted televised paranormal research team to come and investigate for themselves. The team came up with evidence of their own that seemed to support many of the claims of guests and witnesses. At the end of the investigation, the team concluded that there were certainly paranormal forces at work in the two houses. Hopefully I will have an opportunity in the future to investigate this former bed and breakfast for myself. Until that time, it seems that this site of many resting visitors and a "Historic Haunt" may contain occupants in a decidedly un-restful state!

ROOTIN' TOOTIN' SHOOTIN' SPIRITS
Six Gun Territory, Ocala

A Theme Park Says Howdy

Bringing a bit of the "Wild West" to Florida; Six Gun Territory in Ocala, was a complete 1880's style Western town. It had everything the old west was famous for: a jail, a courthouse, a bank, an apothecary, a hat shop (for the ladies), a general store, a Saloon, and so much more. The park tried to give visitors the full Wild West experience. A Saloon hosted realistic "can can" shows every day, outlaws often attacked the train outside of town, and high noon gunfights were staged by stuntmen for the crowd's amusement in the streets and buildings around town. After the shows (or during), visitors could ride the sky ride from one end of the park to the other, take the western train ride, or travel to the Indian village and trading post which represented 32 different Indian tribes. If this wasn't enough, tourists could also head to the Mexican Border Town, where all the food and entertainment you could want was provided from south of the border. The park even contained an area called the Country Fair, where guests could ride the more modern rides and play arcade games.

Six Gun Territory opened February 2nd, 1963 and continued to operate for 20 years. Many tourists included it in their visits to Ocala along with the Silver Springs. As South Florida changed and tourism in other parts of the state grew, this theme park was unable to keep pace with the large parks in Orlando. This was the reason Six Gun territory shut its gates January 1st, 1984. In 1986, the whole area was bulldozed and slated for development except for Six Gun Plaza and Oak Hill Plantation. Leaving barely a trace that Six Gun Territory was ever in existence. Few remnants of the park remain. At one point there were reportedly still signs of the park's railroad track lines still intact, in a wooded area near the new developments. Unfortunately, during my investigation I found no trace of it. The park and its railroad may be gone, but the train ride is one reason why the area is said to still be haunted and the source of several paranormal stories.

Mysterious Train Whistles and Ghostly Gunfighters

While researching this story I did find several references suggesting that a tourist at the old park actually passed away from heat stroke on the train. I wondered if the area could be holding residual energy from someone dying so suddenly. I spoke with several residents who have lived in the subdivision that sprang up in the park's old location. Some have been there for over 25 years. One resident in particular, that I interviewed, told me that neighbors have talked about hearing the train whistle blowing loudly nearby from time to time. According to her, these residents have waited to see signs of some kind of train after hearing the nearby whistle and were surprised to see none. Many residents went further, claiming the area where Six Gun Territory used to be is haunted. Having long since grown accustomed to the mysterious train whistle, they jokingly refer to it as the ghost train.

In my research I also came across reports suggesting that other deaths had taken place here at Six Gun Territory. Most of these reports mentioned accidents involving

60

the gun fighting stuntmen, among others. There are so many contradictory stories about possible deaths at the park and their causes that I just didn't know what to believe. This wouldn't be the first time a theme park has buried or down played details of accidents or deaths (and it probably won't be the last). It's hard to ignore these reports, as they may explain the many witnesses who have reported hearing screams in the woods where the train once traveled. Further investigation, however, has revealed nothing.

The local woman I interviewed also told me about how her husband used to take nature walks through the woods until he heard gun shots. He went back to the house and called the police. The police came and searched the area finding nothing. The man claimed he heard several gun shots, but never saw anything. A few days later around the same time (noon) he heard the shots again. He went back to the house, and again called the police. They came back out and searched the area, again finding nothing. The investigating officers told the man that they have often had calls like this before; someone hears gun shots always around noon. Maybe the gun fighters are still returning for the staged shoot out that took place at high noon? The police claimed there was an increase in reports of these mysterious mid-day gunshots just after the theme park closed. Local residents, who experienced the sounds, claim they haven't heard them in a long time. The gun fight seems to have quieted down, but reports of the train whistle blowing still persist.

While in town, researching a few other locations in the area, I spoke to other locals about Six Gun Territory. One woman I spoke with said that her uncle used to work there and was a gun fighter. He went to the area where the park used to be right after it closed and swore he still heard the train whistle. This occurred when the park was abandoned, right before the wrecking ball arrived to start taking everything down. The train had long ago been moved to Texas, but he distinctly heard the whistle sound. Having worked there for years, there was no mistaking the train's familiar whistle. The woman's uncle also told her several stories about the gun fighters who worked at the park. Interestingly enough, they claimed while alive that if there was an afterlife they would surely return to Six Gun Territory for their High Noon Shoot Outs.

To this day many people who walk through the woods off Highway 40, in the area where Six Gun Territory once stood, make many claims, not only of ghostly gunshots and eerie whistles, but of an uneasy feeling that comes over them the longer they stay on the old park's site. I too felt this uncomfortable sensation when visiting the site and so did another witness I brought for the investigation. Perhaps these locals and I should have tipped our hats and paid our respects to this former "Historic Haunt"?

Postcard from the park's heyday | Author's Collection

GHOSTLY SENSATIONS MADE CRYSTAL CLEAR
Soul Essentials Crystal & Gift Shop, Ocala

Soul Essentials Crystal & Gift Shop | Photo: Author

Drawn to Ms. Burke's place

Crystals are affected by paranormal energies. They have been repeatedly shown to have some sort of connection to these types of energies and activities. Despite being dismissed by many as merely decorative elements or new wave "mumbo jumbo"; many people seem to acknowledge this connection and support it. Some even open shops dedicated to these mysterious rocks. Jennifer Burke has one of the most beautiful crystal shops I've ever seen. The store is situated in a beautiful old Victorian home that was built in 1915. It has a lot of character, and an unusual feel to it. I was visiting Ocala investigating a couple of other locations when I came across her shop. I was intrigued by this old building and it was almost as if it had its own energy and was pulling me towards it.

As I roamed through the house I asked Jennifer if she lived in the house as well and she said "yes". In fact, she lived upstairs. I lived in St. Augustine at the time and we discussed how great it was to live so close to work, and how you could work late without having to travel far to get home.

The Three Spirits

Still smiling from our friendly chat, I left Jennifer and went into another room. This was the main room where customers check out with their purchases. As soon as I entered I felt very much at peace, like a person who had walked into the comfort of their grandmother's home. Coincidentally, this thought occurred to me just as I felt the presence of an older woman there in the room with me. I turned (thinking someone had to have entered the room behind me) and found myself alone. I decided to go back to the room where Jennifer was busily unpacking crystal bowls and ask her who the elderly woman was. She was caught by surprise with my comment and asked me, "Did you see her?" Instead of answering directly I commented, "So the place IS haunted right?" She replied, "Yes, very much so." She informed me that many people have seen, heard, and felt the presence of an elderly woman in the home; especially in the same room where I first experienced her. This spirit is believed to be the former owner who doesn't want to leave, and just wants to keep an eye on things. A peaceful spirit, her appearance always leaves people feeling a great sense of contentment.

I asked her if she had experienced anything else in the house and she told me about the spirit of a small child that plays upstairs, especially in one particular room. When Jennifer first moved in, the child would get into boxes and move things around. From Jennifer's vivid descriptions it sounded as if she was looking for something to play with like toys. The spirit loves to play and string stuff all around the room. Many witnesses believe this may have been her room when she was living in the house. Jennifer went on to tell me that the young girl passed at an early age due to illness. She informed me that many people have felt the presence of a child in the house before they've even heard the story about the ghost.

After Jennifer shared the story about the child, I felt the need to ask about the other spirit I was sensing. I asked if there was a man here too and her expression changed. She was very serious as she described a rather tall, domineering man with a dark mustache. He had been seen by many people and gave off a menacing energy (the same feeling I got from him). She didn't go into much detail about him except to say she once heard him call her a "not so nice name" and that he made her a little uncomfortable. I asked her if the man's spirit has some attachment to the back exterior stair case, because it had a negative feel to me. She wasn't sure about the male spirit's connection to the staircase, but she didn't like the energy back there either, so she had blocked off the doorway! My suspicions confirmed, I returned to the peaceful calm of the checkout room.

Located as it is, right down the street from the old Seven Sisters Bed & Breakfast (another "Historic Haunt"), Jennifer's place has great neighbors. Soul Essentials is a beautiful shop in a fantastically restored historic home. Unfortunately, I was on a tight schedule that day, which prevented me from making a detailed examination of the building (although I still felt it was noteworthy and hope to get back there soon). Still, considering the fact that my trip was actually to investigate other locations in Ocala; discovering Jennifer Burke's place was an unexpected bonus!

THE GHOSTLY SPRING
Silver Springs Park, Ocala

Clearly a Natural Wonder

What goes on just below the surface? I think we are all curious about taking a peek from time to time and learning what goes on just below the water. Before the invention of SCUBA gear and underwater cameras, Silver Springs Zoological Park, located in the Silver Springs River State Park banked on this common interest. Visitors were drawn here in the 1870's, because of the amazing attraction of their glass bottom boats. People could float along the springs in a boat with a transparent bottom and see all the beauty that the springs and its aquatic life offered. The park quickly became a popular attraction. In 1880, former President Ulysses S. Grant even visited here, sharing an interest in this new attraction at the springs with the others who came to visit.

As time went on the park's reputation only grew. Colonel Tooey, the concessionaire who operated the Jungle Cruise Boat Ride tried to establish the first troop of wild rhesus monkeys here in the 1930's. He was hoping to attract more visitors to his famed Jungle Cruise, but the rhesuses were good swimmers and escaped. The monkeys were later found in feral groups along the river. Descendents of this group can still be seen on the tours.

Silver Spring's glass bottom boats, clear waters and beautiful park continued to draw visitors in droves. Some of these visitors came from Hollywood. Several movies and television shows have used Silver Springs as their beautiful scenic backdrop. In the 1930's, Tarzan was filmed here. The studio, like Colonel Tooey, brought monkeys to the area to be in these episodes. Like he Colonel, some of these primates escaped into the wilds of Silver Springs. During the 70's, "The Six Million Dollar Man" and some under water scenes from early James Bond movies were filmed here as well.

The Ghosts of the Indian Lovers

Many of the paranormal stories associated with this area occur in the region called "The Bridal Chamber". There have been reports for years at Silver Springs of two commonly seen manifestations. A male and a female apparition have been spotted by many witnesses in the water of The Bridal Chamber, in the middle of a warm embrace. During my interviews I spoke to a long time Silver Springs employee (now retired) who was able to shed some light on these reports and the legendary tales associated with the area. According to the legend, every so many years, Indians would come to the area from all over for peace camps. They would meet at the shores of Blue Run (which is now known as Silver Springs).

The legend continues with by describing a very beautiful Indian maiden who had caught everyone's eye. The Indians who saw her fell in love with her. While the Indians attended their peace camp, she would sit along a crooked palm that reached over the springs, watching the games the other Indians were playing. As she watched the others playing, she was suddenly pushed into the water. She swam back up through the water enraged and wanting to know who had shoved her into the springs. There, on the bank of the river, was a handsome Seminole Indian holding his hand out, waiting to help her to shore. He told her that her life was now his. She inquired angrily how and why he could think such a thing. He informed her that according to tribal law, when one saves another's life, they then owe their lives to one another.

The handsome young Seminole continued by telling her that he had pushed her into that water for a good reason. There was a cotton mouth snake in the tree behind her, which would have struck had he not pushed her out of the tree. If he had taken the time to warn her, she would have been bitten. The young brave then claimed he killed the snake by stabbing it through the head with his knife. He took the young princess to see the snake which was dead in the tree with his knife through its head.

The legend goes on to say that the couple fell in love. Not everyone was happy, another Indian warrior had feelings for the young princess, but she never returned those feelings. He felt the Seminole Indian had stolen her love from him. One dark night, the jealous Indian brave hid in the bushes waiting for the young Seminole to return home. As the young warrior walked by he jumped out of the bushes and struck him over the head with a strong blow from a large rock. The Princess' true love died the next day in her arms from the head wound. Before he died, he told her that he was truly blessed by her love, even though he had only experienced it for a short period of time. According to the legend, the brave also cast a spell on the old crooked palm tree. He claimed that anyone who meets and falls in love in this area of the springs will be granted a love that will last forever. After his death, the Indian brave was weighted and thrown into the deepest part of the springs.

The story continues, with the princess becoming so depressed that she refused to live without her love. She found a strong vine and tied it around her neck, fastening the other end to a heavy rock. She pushed the rock in and jumped into the springs to be with her true love. Anchored to the rock, she disappeared out of site into the depths of the reportedly bottomless spring. As soon as she disappeared, a burst of white lime rock bubbled to the top of the springs. The legend claims this is why you can still see white lime rock bubble to the surface.

As for the murderer, no one knows exactly what happened to the Indian who killed the young Seminole, but according to the legend he is still at the springs looking for eternal peace. A peace which he cannot have because of the heinous murder he committed.

If these legends contain any truth, than this means that there could be at least three spirits still in the area. The lovers are said to still be in a passionate embrace, and the murderer is still haunting the grounds. Oddly enough, most of the paranormal activity reported and sightings seem to back this legend up! During my last visit to Silver Springs, I felt warmth near the crooked palm that reminded me of the love and passion of the young couple. Other eyewitnesses have described a similar sensation in this area. It was a feeling that they were at peace happily spending their afterlife together. I have yet to personally encounter the sightings that so many people reported of the young lovers or the wandering Indian. There is definitely a strong feeling of happiness and peace emanating from the area around the crooked palm. Perhaps when I return, I will sneak my equipment to this Historic Haunt and the couple will allow me to share in their happiness.

THE UNLUCKY AND UNUSUAL LIGHTHOUSE
Ponce de Leon Inlet Lighthouse, Ponce Inlet

The Unlucky Beacon

For many sailors lighthouses were a lifeline. Their existence helped lessen the chance of crashing on the rocks in tricky coastline areas and inlet. The residents of the area once known as Mosquito Inlet, saw the need to help seafarers and the first lighthouse was erected in 1835. The lighthouse seemed to have the odds stacked against it from the onset, as oil was never delivered to Ponce De Leon Inlet, and soon after the tower was completed, a strong storm washed much of the sand from the base causing the tower to eventually weaken.

In December of 1835, the Second Seminole War began, and Seminole Indians attacked the lighthouse, busting the glass and setting the wooden stairs a blaze. After the attack the area was abandoned, and the tower collapsed the following year. The inlet spent many years with no lighthouse. As a result of the coast being in the dark many ships wrecked along the coast. It wasn't until 1883 that an effort was made to place another light on the inlet.

Construction was to begin under the supervision of Chief Engineer Orville E. Babcock until he drowned in Mosquito Inlet in 1884. The project dragged for three years, but endured, even surviving the Charleston Earthquake of 1886. The new lighthouse was completed and lit in 1887, and could be seen for 20 miles out into the Atlantic Ocean. The structure stood (as it does today) 203 steps to the top and 159 feet tall.

Not long after it began service, the lighthouse helped save many lives, including that of Stephen Crane (author of The Red Badge of Courage). The original lamp burned with kerosene until 1909, when it was replaced with an incandescent oil vapor lamp. In 1927, Mosquito Inlet was renamed Ponce de Leon Inlet for the purposes of tourism and real estate. In 1933, the lighthouse was electrified with a 500 watt electric lamp. In 1939, the lighthouse was transferred into Coast Guard Service. With the onset of World War II, the keeper's houses were converted into barracks for Coast Guardsmen who maintained the lights and watched the coast for enemy submarines. Late in 1953, well after the war, the lighthouse became completely automated. In 1970, the Coast Guard established a new light station on the south side of the inlet. The old lighthouse sat abandoned and vandalized, until the Ponce de Leon Inlet Lighthouse Preservation Association became involved in 1972. This non-profit group set out to restore and operate the property as a museum. The Light Station became listed on the National Register of Historic Places. Through continued efforts by this group of dedicated volunteers, a full restoration was completed in stages during 1982, 1995, 2003 and 2004. This stoic, but historic beauty, is now officially listed as an "operational private aid to navigation"

The Ponce's Paranormal Visitors

In its time of service the lighthouse saw several keepers. One Sunday in October 1919, assistant light keeper Joseph Davis was filling in for the Principal Keeper. Davis

66

had to carry a heavy bucket of kerosene fuel up to the top of the tower to refuel the beacon. As he reached the 7th landing he suffered his third and final heart attack and died on the landing. The smell of kerosene in the tower wasn't considered unusual until it continued long after the tower was electrified in 1933. Even after the conversion the kerosene smell would still reportedly manifest itself every night just before dusk. Some in the paranormal field suggest that Joseph Davis is still maintaining the light. So many light keepers' spirits seem to return to their lighthouses after their death, still wanting to do their duties keeping ships at sea safe and sound.

Ponce de Leon Inlet Lighthouse

Photo: Author

Another ghost many witnesses have reported residing here at the lighthouse is the son of another light keeper. Tom Hagen was keeper here during the first decade of the 20th century. Hagen's son was kicked in the head by a horse. He died from the severe injuries. The spirit of Hagen's son seems to be lingering not only in the tower, but also in the keeper's house. Witnesses have reported the sounds of small footsteps and giggling, which can be heard throughout the tower. Opening and closing doors have been heard in the keeper's house and employees have reported childish pranks being played on them during the day and night. The most common of these pranks being certain objects, which are moved from one place to another or disappearing, only to reappear later in another place.

The last time I visited Ponce Inlet Lighthouse I smelled the distinct smell of kerosene, and thinking the lighthouse was electric, asked the historian on duty, if the lighthouse was still lit the old fashioned way. He assured me the light had been electrified years ago, and that everyone at the museum was convinced the old keeper's spirit doesn't realize it is and still tries to do it the old way. The historian there on the grounds, seems to think that Davis' spirit is a residual one. Reports indicate that when he appears he just continues to do the same thing over and over, and never interacts with anyone.

After climbing the tower, I went through the keeper's quarters, and heard the sounds of little feet running through the other room. I figured there must be a visiting family group touring in the other room. The sounds from the other room grew louder and made conversation difficult. I made the comment to a friend I'd brought on my research trip that I was going to stick my head in the doorway, and see how many kids were running around. As I poked my head through the door way, I discovered there was no one there; we were the only two people in the keeper's house! I came back into the room and asked my friend "You did hear all that didn't you?" He replied, "Heck yeah, did they leave?" I replied, "There was no one there!"

I examined the layout of the house and determined that no one could have been next door and left without leaving a trace or making loud sounds of departure. My experience and those of my assistant seemed to verify the reports and experiences of so many at the lighthouses site. The Ponce de Leon Inlet Lighthouse seems to be one of Florida's most remarkable Historic Haunts, and one I intend to investigate further.

"A ROUGH ROAD LEADS TO THE STARS"
Apollo 1 Launch Pad 34 Kennedy Space Center
....

An American Tragedy

Apollo 1 was scheduled to be the first manned mission of the Apollo Program and was to be launched on February 21st, 1967. On January 27th, 1967, at launch pad 34, during a launch pad test, a cabin fire erupted inside Apollo 1 which killed the entire 3 man crew. Command Pilot Virgil "Gus" Grissom, Senior Pilot Edward White, and Pilot Roger Chaffee were all lost to the fire. It was one of the first and greatest tragedies of the space program, and an important historic moment in America's quest to reach the stars.

Launch Pad 34   Photo: Author

The Paranormal and Pad 34

Many in the paranormal field believe that tragic events can leave a residual energy. It is an energy that sometimes leads to spiritual manifestations and Apollo, no doubt certainly qualifies. Many visitors to Pad 34 at Kennedy Space Center have reported paranormal experiences. Visitors to the site have heard screams of terror coming from this area when there is no one around. They've also seen apparitions running around the launch site. Many have theorized that it may be the energy of the crew trying to put out the fire in a desperate attempt to save the unlucky astronauts. For a time, NASA had reportedly excluded Pad 34 from their tours due to these reported "strange occurrences".

My Experiences on the Launch Pad

I had heard about the paranormal experiences at Launch Pad 34. To my surprise, while researching this book, I took the Cape Canaveral "Then and Now" Tour. The Apollo 1 launch site was once again included. As I walked closer and closer to the launch pad, I could feel the air getting heavier and heavier. It was a pervading feeling of dread and sorrow. The Florida weather was unseasonably cool and it wasn't hot out, but the closer I got to the launch site the warmer and warmer I felt. When I eventually stood in the middle of launch pad 34, the sensation became so extreme that I felt as if I was on fire. I was sweating profusely and quite unnerved. It became so bad that I moved away from the unnatural heat and towards the plaque near the site. I began reading the plaque on the launch pad telling the story of this great disaster and

68

was suddenly overcome with the sensation that someone was standing behind me. I turned around and there was no one there. The entire tour had moved to the other side of the launch site. As I moved to join them I couldn't shake this heavy feeling of grief that had come over me. I reached the rest of the tour group and felt compelled to ask the tour guides about the paranormal reports I'd researched and my own recent uncomfortable experience. Rumors had leaked to me that tour guides were prohibited from discussing these "strange occurrences" paranormal or otherwise. I was only moderately surprised when I posed my questions privately to one of the guides and watched him become uncomfortable, suddenly growing rigid and wide-eyed. What surprised me more was how abruptly he turned and walked away from me without answering? When I mentioned ghosts at Kennedy again (later in the tour bus), the bus driver quickly and suspiciously averted his eyes and turned his head. The tour guide, meanwhile, quickly changed the subject by calling out over my head for the rest of the tour to regroup.

A Personal Note on the Tragedy

I was on hand at one of the causeways during the tragedy of the 1986 Challenger. It was a horrific personal experience I will likely never forget. Standing there near Pad 34, I felt a connection with everyone that experienced that terrible day in January 1967. Apollo's astronauts (like those of Challenger), should remain an important part of American history and shouldn't be forgotten by the public or by visitors to Kennedy. Despite the fact that Kennedy Space Center reportedly once took Launch Pad 34 off the tour, I was pleased to find that it had apparently been reintroduced. It is truly an amazing piece of Florida's history and a testament to man's pioneering efforts!

The plaque at Launch Pad 34.
May they never be forgotten

Photo: Author

69

GHOSTLY CAPTIVES OF THE COURT
Orange County Courthouse, Orlando

A History of Justice

The original Orange County Courthouse is on East Central Boulevard. It has been renamed the Orange County History Center. This early courthouse was built in 1927. For 71 years this building was used as the county courthouse, before a new one was built. There are many stories displayed here in the museum from Orange County's

The former Orange County Courthouse   Photo: Author

past. A past before the mega theme parks took over, and a perspective of Orlando that is shown from as far back as 200 years ago. However, with all the history of Orlando shared with its many visitors, it can be easy to forget that this building too has a history, and a few noteworthy stories of its own.

The Most Famous Guest of the State

During its long history, the courthouse has seen many visitors, employees, prisoners, and killers, but perhaps it's most famous "guest of the state" was Ted Bundy! On January 7th, 1980, serial killer Ted Bundy was tried here for murdering Kimberly Leach. He was found guilty exactly one month later. During the trial he was reportedly so filled with rage over the proceedings that he carved his name in the table he was sitting at during the trial. Before his execution and during the trial, Bundy was housed on the 5th floor where the jail cells were located. Ted Bundy's trial and execution may have stirred up several ghosts from the past, but his own ghost is apparently not one. In my research, reports of his spirit haunting or affecting this building were happily non-existent. Instead, there have been several other reports about the building detailing other paranormal encounters. Even if Bundy's ghost is not there, the actual old courtroom seems to be where most of the activity takes place.

The Girl and the Guard

One spirit that many witnesses have reported is named Emily. She was a little girl that was caught in the middle of the Orange County Foster Care system, and unfortunately, died at a very early age. Many people claim to have felt her presence or encountered her personally. She seems to be more attracted to men, possibly still

70

searching for a father figure to comfort her.

Another ghost reported frequently is that of an ex jail guard named Frank. I uncovered many reports that would indicate that he still seems to be on duty watching the prisoners. Reports of noises and movement coming from the old jail area seem to support many people's claims. This may also explain why Frank is apparently still on the job. Whether he is a residual haunt, continuing his rounds or an active presence who feels compelled to keep an eye on other spirits (or those of long passed prisoners) has not yet been determined.

During my first visit here, I knew absolutely nothing about the building, or its history of ghosts. I came to the former courthouse as a tourist to experience the history of Orange County. As I entered into the old courtroom I could just feel the air change. Like many haunted sites I've encountered, the barometric pressure just seemed to drop in this room. A room, I discovered later, where Emily and Frank are often both reported to be seen. As I proceeded farther into the room, and looked around, I was surprised to see a dark shadow darting into a doorway that once led to the judge's chambers. There were no other people around me to have cast the shadow, and certainly none moving that fast. The shadow disappeared even as I moved closer to investigate. Needless to say my curiosity was piqued and after my visit I began further researching the building and its related stories. I discovered there were many reports surrounding this now marvelous museum, but not as many details as in other sites I'd encountered. Still I refuse to give up my research. There is a lot of mystery about the paranormal inhabitants of the former Orange County Courthouse. While I may not have served enough time there yet to thoroughly research it; I feel compelled to find it guilty on two counts. The first is being an amazing museum for kids and adults with fascinating exhibits, the second is being one of Florida's more intriguing "Historic Haunts".

PARANORMAL PACHYDERMS
Circus World, Haines City

A History of Greasepaint and Guests

Ringling's Circus World | Photo: Author

Everyone loves the circus. In 1973, the owners of Ringling Brothers and Barnum and Bailey Circus were counting on this when they started to build Circus World Showcase, a fantastic theme park centered on a circus theme. The park, located on US 27, just east of Interstate 4, was supposedly the first stage of a new "Circus World" theme park. This new park, when completed, would not only provide the circus itself with new winter quarters, but would also contain circus based rides and shows.

Circus World opened in February 1974 with a 27,000 square foot structure that resembled a big top! It was the biggest circus big top tent anyone had ever seen. The showcase also featured an IMAX theater, a model of the fully proposed park, and circus memorabilia displays. A show was later added to allow guests to try walking a tightrope or flying on the trapeze (all with safety equipment). The decision was soon made to drop "Showcase" from the name.

The park had a rocky life, being farther south, it was having trouble competing against the mega theme parks in Orlando. In the late 1970's Felds (the current owners of the circus), sold the circus off to Mattel, the noted toymaker and Barbie producer. Mattel was actually hoping to sell the park, but with no interested parties, decided to move ahead with expansion plans to make it more enticing. By 1982, work to revamp the circus began. They decided to add more than just clowns, tight rope walkers, and side show acts. Animal shows were made bigger and better and thrill rides were added. The Roaring Tiger, the largest wooden roller coaster in the area, was designed to attract thrill seekers from all over, as was the Flying Daredevil (an Arrow shuttle loop). They also built the world's largest elephant barn, a petting zoo, children's area and added more carnival rides. With these new additions, they believed their tourism numbers would rise quickly. The further addition of landscaping, a giant Ferris wheel, and a looping coaster did little to turn the park's fortunes around. In 1986, the park was sold to a publishing group who envisioned a rebirth for their park.

New Owners Play Ball

Their idea was a totally new theme park, Boardwalk and Baseball. The circus concept was played down and the concept of a turn of the century seaside boardwalk was played up. Circus displays were taken away to make way for Cooperstown exhibits.

72

North of the park, a baseball stadium was built, and the Kansas City Royals were lured away from their normal Grapefruit League headquarters in Ft. Myers with promises of huge crowds of tourists. The park was very nice, but being out of the flow of tourists, south of Orlando, it never quite took hold. The park was sold again to Busch Entertainment (who already owned and operated Busch Gardens about an hour away). They maintained Boardwalk and Baseball for a short time before pulling the plug in January of 1990. The life span of the baseball theme park was even shorter lived than Circus World. They just couldn't compete with the millions of tourist dollars in Orlando.

A few years went by and the property sold yet again. But what would go in next? A huge development: including condos, hotels, offices and a shopping center. But there are still a few remnants of Circus World left. They aren't just visible.

The Elephant Not in the Room

During Circus World's heyday, animals from the show sometimes passed away due to age or illness. They were buried upon their deaths there on the grounds. A few employees working in the shopping center have reported strange experiences, both sight and sound. One person I interviewed who works in one of the retail stores there shared an experience with me. He said that he was walking out to his

Circus World's Elephant Show | Photo: Author

car late one night after he got off of work, tired and ready to go home. As he approached his car he saw something off in the distance, and couldn't figure out what it was. He decided to walk closer to try to figure out what it was. As he approached he did a double take, it was an elephant! After he realized what he was seeing he decided to try and get closer to it. The closer he got the more the apparition started to dissipate before eventually disappearing altogether. After his experience he doubted what he had witnessed. Until one day while on break, one of his female coworkers asked him if he ever saw anything weird late at night near the parking lot. Before he could tell his story, she described her experience with an almost identical progression of events. They discovered they weren't the only ones to have experienced the ghostly elephants, other employees at the shopping center reported similar encounters. Some have even reported hearing the sounds of an elephant trumpeting, especially late at night, when few people were around.

Animal spirits have been reported in many cases, and they can return from their graves just the same as humans have. I was not surprised to hear that people had seen elephants roaming the grounds considering they lived and worked there too. It's a shame that Circus World is no longer in existence. It was a brilliant idea, and a fantastic piece of early Florida that we, like the elephants, should never forget.

73

THE SPIRITED SPOOK HILL
Spook Hill, Lake Wales

The Indian & the Alligator

If you make it to central Florida and you don't visit Spook Hill you've missed out! North Wales Drive is where you can find this local roadside attraction. Spook Hill is practically world renowned, having been featured in prominent newspapers, and television programs. A natural phenomenon like this, often has associated claims of unusual or supernatural forces. But Spook Hill has an awesome legend attached to it, which is officially recognized by the town of Lake Wales.

Historians know there was a Calusas Indian Village here at Lake Wales. The legend claims that the leader of the tribe was Chief Cufcowellax, a great, well respected, and powerful man. His tribe lived here peacefully until one day when the town was plagued by a massive bull alligator. The gator was raiding the entire Indian village. To save his people, and the village, Chief Cufcowellax set out to find and kill this horrible beast. He searched for days, and when he finally found the huge reptile, the battle began. The legend claims that the battle went on for several days as the chief's tribesmen looked on. Finally, the great chief succeeded in killing the alligator. Some say a lake appeared after the battle from all the blood that was shed and others say the battle took place at the edge of the lake. The latter of these being most plausible. This local legend became intertwined with the special qualities of this unusual site.

Natural Phenomenon or ghost?

By the turn of the century, pioneer mail riders and horse drawn carriages seem to labor severely going DOWN the hill. This baffled the townsfolk. Why would anyone or anything labor traveling downhill? Many people believed it was caused by the spirit of the chief watching over his village. Others believed it was the spirit of the angry alligator seeking revenge on the town. Regardless, there have been several instances of people hearing guttural sounds as if an alligator were close by when in fact there were no animals around. There are also eyewitnesses who report actually seeing Chief Cufcowellax, walking around the area where Spook Hill is located. Having researched these reports, it seems the "spook" at Spook Hill may not be limited to the optical illusion of the hill. There may, in fact, be spooks of another sort here!

Experience it for Yourself

Drive to Spook Hill; follow the directions on the sign (at the foot of the hill). Park your car on the line, and put it in neutral, and don't be surprised when your car appears to roll up the hill. Also try placing a ball in the center of the street, at the line, and watch it roll up hill as well.

These types of anomalies once baffled scientists for decades. Mystery hills occur when the geography of an area produces the optical illusion that a slight downhill slope seems to be an uphill slope. Ghosts, legend, and optical illusion, Spook Hill is a pretty interesting piece of historic Florida and a fun natural attraction. If you see a large angry alligator I'd suggest you run, but make sure it's not uphill.

THE HAUNTED FISHING VILLAGE AND THE BOMBER PILOT

Boatyard Village, Clearwater

....

A Clearwater Landmark

I remember going to Boatyard Village as a little kid. It captured my imagination even as a child. I thought it was the coolest place. It was like going back in time to another era. Even then I loved history and historic looking places. Boatyard Village was built to look like an 1890's or early 1900's, fishing village. Old docks followed along the water with quaint little

Boatyard Village | Photo: David MacLean

shops and restaurants to enjoy. It truly had the feeling of a bye gone era. My mom used to take me there when I was little to walk the docks, look in the stores, and have lunch at the restaurant with the huge Coca Cola sign on the outside wall.

My Experiences at Boatyard Village and With the Captain

One of the earliest experiences I had at the village, involved a time when I was walking on the dock ahead of my mom. I turned the corner and caught a glimpse of the faint shadowy figure of a man in old style clothing. The short moment after I saw him he vanished. I didn't even have time to turn to my mom and tell her to look. I barely remember seeing the details and quickly tried to describe this man to her. Since those early days, I have spoken to several other people who lived in the area and remember visiting there. A few of them described seeing a similar shadowy figure of a man, in period dress, who was gone as quickly as they saw him.

My family and I lived at the time, in the vicinity of Boatyard Village. The private school I went to even took us here once on a field trip. Included in our tour was the Military Aviation Museum just across the way. As a child, another fascination I had was with flying! I loved looking at the old airplanes and imaging where they had been and what battles they might have fought. Oh the stories those planes could tell. For me, this was one of the best field trips EVER! The museum housed 9 planes and one in particular that I was drawn to. I wasn't alone; there was a small group of students, like me, curious about investigating one particular plane. The plane was a B52 Bomber, and it exerted a strong pull on all of us. As the other kids were walking around, and under the plane, I found myself staring into the cockpit. The longer I

75

looked, the more I realized there was a hazy form coalescing into a man sitting in the cockpit, looking back at me. He had a military uniform on and a cap. We made eye contact. At first I thought it was a museum employee, a re-enactor portraying an old military pilot. I looked up at him more intensely trying to distinguish more details; he looked down at me with equal intensity. He nodded his head at me, smiled, and tipped his hat. I waved up at him and smiled, and then he was gone! None of the others seemed to notice him; they were too busy running around the plane playing. I remember asking one of the other kids about it, hoping they had seen him as I had. The other student looked at me as if I were crazy.

This event stayed with me, and is one of the reasons I grew up and took a job in the paranormal field. As an adult and investigator, I have done more research, discovering several others who like me, witnessed the apparition of a pilot in the same B52 Bomber. Every story I followed seemed to have the same pattern of events. The pilot seems to acknowledge each person and then just vanishes.

Unfortunately, the year 2000 marked the end of the fascinating Boatyard Village. The 17 acres of land that housed the village were reportedly being bought up by the U.S. Army Reserve. The whole area and all traces of Boatyard Village have been demolished. Another quaint road side attraction, no longer with us, and another "Historic Haunt" gone!

A TRAGIC CROSSING
Sunshine Skyway Bridge, Tampa Bay
....

A History of Tragedies and Loss of Life

There are many people who suffer from a deathly fear of bridges. Members of the medical profession have termed this condition, gephyrophobia. Perhaps these fears are justified when a bridge has been surrounded by as many tragic moments as the Skyway Bridge over Tampa Bay. The original Skyway Bridge was a cantilever bridge spanning Tampa Bay, connecting St. Petersburg to Sarasota. The two lane bridge was built by The Virginia Bridge Company in 1954. In 1969, construction began on a similar bridge parallel to the current one with the intent of combining the two bridges and making a 4

lane structure. This second bridge was completed, but its opening was delayed due to the need for reinforcing the south main pier (after it cracked due to insufficient supporting pile depth). The structure, finally brought to Interstate standards, opened for service in 1971, one span was designated for northbound

postcard of the Sunshine Skyway Bridge | Author's Collection

traffic and the other for southbound traffic.

The string of tragedies started in 1980, when on January 28th, the U.S. Coast Guard Cutter *Blackthorn* was heading outbound from Tampa Bay and the tanker *Capricorn* was heading inbound. A third vessel, an approaching cruise ship was also in the bay with all its lights running on deck. The lights were so bright that the *Blackthorn* noticed and moved into the middle of the channel out of the vessel's way. The pilots of the *Blackthorn* moved out of the cruise ship's way and into the middle of the channel, still blinded by the lights, and didn't immediately see the *Capricorn* until it was heading directly towards them. The *Blackthorn* quickly signaled to the *Capricorn* to pass on the starboard side, but the *Capricorn* was crowding the center part of the channel. The two ships collided nearly head on. Six crewmen onboard the *Blackthorn* were trapped by the mangled metal skin of the ship. The *Blackthorn* was damaged further when the *Capricorn's* anchor was imbedded in its hull. The two ship's momentum carried them along the anchor line which pulled taut and capsized the *Blackthorn*. Twenty three men drowned that day trapped on board and below decks as the Skyway Bridge nearby standing a solemn vigil. Because of the fatal accidents on the

77

Blackthorn, the decision was made to strip the ship of its gear, and sell her for spare parts instead of repairing her and putting her back out to sea. The hull was even towed offshore and intentionally sunk to make an artificial reef.

A second tragedy involving the bridge occurred that same year on a stormy, rainy May 9th. News reports broke into all television programs to announce that the freighter *Summit Venture*, another large vessel, had destroyed the southbound span at 7:30 a.m. when it collided with a support column during the terrible storm. These reports went on to say that after its radar failed, the ship was unable to overcome the storm with its intense fog, heavy rains, thunder, lightning and tropical storm force winds. The *Summit* took down over 1200 feet of the bridge and it fell into Tampa Bay. Along with the bridge, ten cars and a Greyhound bus fell over 150 feet into the Bay. Thirty-five people perished that day. Wesley MacIntire was the only survivor, when his vehicle bounced off the freighter, breaking its fall somewhat, before it struck the water. The next nine remaining years of his life he was haunted by the accident, wondering why he was the only survivor that horrible day. MacIntire succumbed to bone cancer in 1989, but received some solace as he and his wife were the last to drive over the old Sunshine Skyway Bridge. When they reached the highest point of the bridge they got out of their car, and dropped white carnations into the Bay, one for each person who died that day.

The current bridge was built soon after the terrible tragedy involving the *Summit Venture*, and the old bridge was demolished. The new bridge is considered one of the top ten bridges in the world and is hailed by many as Florida's "flag bridge", but even this acclaim does little to improve its tarnished image. In addition to the deaths from these high profile incidents, there have been at least 130 documented suicides to date off the new Skyway Bridge since 1987 and 51 from the old Skyway Bridge. Authorities suggest possibly even more, but can't be certain without bodies. In 1999, a twenty-four hour suicide hotline was started and signs were posted all along the bridge to try to prevent any more suicides from occurring. These efforts have been somewhat successful, but authorities claim it has done little to end the bridge's popularity as a site for committing suicide. Further tragic events related to the bridge include: a failed "pendulum swing" bungee jump that resulted in broken bones and neck injuries for a group of amateur daredevils, and a body found in the trunk of a burning car.

My Personal Experiences & the Ghosts of Soaked Hitchhikers

As a child born in St. Pete, there were several times when I had to cross the Skyway Bridge. I don't suffer from gephyrophobia but that particular bridge always gave me an intensely uneasy feeling. I used to make sure the windows were all rolled up and the doors were locked and I would sink down in my seat whenever we crossed it. I never knew why the bridge terrified me so much, nor learned it was haunted, until years later.

Surprisingly enough, while there were some reports, the majority of the paranormal accounts I unearthed during my research had nothing to do with the tragic boating accidents involving the bridge area. Instead, these reports seemed to center on the many suicides from the bridge. In many of these reports people claim to see a female hitchhiker with blonde hair wearing blue trying to catch a ride. Everyone who has reported stopping to pick her up, described her as very quiet, and in every instance, as soon as they get to the other side of the bridge she just disappears.

Another common and similar story, centers on a truck driver who stopped to pick up a young woman in a nightgown. When the woman got into the truck, she asked the driver to please drop her at the other side of the bridge. As the truck driver was crossing the bridge he realized the woman was soaking wet! Like the previous report of the other phantom hitchhiker, as soon as the driver got across the bridge, the woman vanished from his vehicle (the driver's story was later printed in the newspaper). Based on these ghostly reports and descriptions, many have speculated that the women could be suicide victims that jumped from the bridge. Their identities remain a mystery, but witnesses continue to come forward with similar claims of encountering them to this day.

While researching this book I went out to the new Skyway Bridge to try to learn more about it and conquer my fear of it. As I stared at that bridge, and drew closer, an overwhelming knot of fear, pain and loss suddenly gripped me. I couldn't get any closer, there's something about that historic bridge and this area that still haunts me.

THE PINK LADY
The Vinoy, St. Petersburg

The Vinoy | Photo: Author

The History of the Pink Lady

In the early 1900's, you were nobody unless you stayed at the Vinoy Hotel in St. Petersburg! Nicknamed the "Pink Lady", the hotel was built in 1925, by Aymer Vinoy Laughner. She was open from December to March, and was the highest priced hotel in town for that time at $20 per night. The hotel contained a light tower in the main part of the building, which would be lit when the hotel was open for business. Seafarers and weary travelers would see the light, and know they could come into port and find a room for the night.

During World War II, the hotel was taken over by the U.S. Army and used for a training school. The hotel's history was rather quiet until she closed from 1974 until the 1990's. It has since been bought by a private company, and undergone a $93,000,000 renovation, the result of which is seven floors of absolute beauty, and a hotel restored to her old glory days.

A Grand Old Haunt

There have been many paranormal encounters reported at this beautiful old hotel. The 4th floor seems to be the most active. A woman in a white dress, and a gentleman in a top hat, has both frequently been seen there wearing attire from the 1940's. These

80

reports seem to indicate that the two do not interact with each other; instead, they both go about their business oblivious of one another.

The lady in white has also been seen on the 5th floor. Evidence would suggest that she may be the spirit of Elsie Elliott, a former socialite who visited the hotel frequently. Her husband Eugene reportedly pushed her down a flight of stairs to her death at the hotel. Further reports and descriptions seem to suggest that Elsie's maid Annie Gadsden, manifests here as well, caring for Mrs. Elliott, even in her afterlife.

Although the 4th floor has the most reported sightings in general, Room# 504 seems to have the most activity in the entire hotel. Among the commonly reported occurrences are apparitions being seen on a frequent basis, doors opening and closing on their own accord, cold spots being felt, and voices heard in the room. The entire fifth floor seems to be a paranormal melting pot.

During my investigation I spoke with one of the hotel front desk attendants. He confided in me the details about visiting opponents of the Tampa Bay professional baseball team. The players (who are often prone to superstition) have all heard the stories about the hotel being haunted, and often times request NOT to be put on the fifth floor. They will even go so far as to share a room with other players rather than staying on the 5th floor. Visiting the Vinoy, while researching this book, I never encountered any apparitions, but one thing I did notice while I was there was a major temperature fluctuation on the 5th floor. There was at least a 10 degree temperature difference than any other floor in the hotel. This was interesting since the hotel maintains a close control of the temperature on each floor.

One housekeeper I spoke with actually carries her rosary with her when she cleans the rooms because she is frightened by the man on the 4th floor. She told me she has seen apparitions of the man and the woman, but the man seems to scare her. She also reported experiencing her cleaning cart being moved all the way to the other end of the hallway; things disappearing off the cart and then reappearing some time later. The woman told me that nothing bad has ever happened to her, but whenever the man's spirit is near, she feels very uneasy and usually goes to another area till she thinks he has gone.

The house keeper told me when Mrs. Elliot is around she always has a sense of peace. I asked her how she knew it was Mrs. Elliot and she told me, "I just know." Don't just take my word for it (or the housekeeper's). I'm not the only one to have investigated this grand old hotel. The Vinoy was visited a few years ago by a popular televised ghost hunting team. They experienced some unusual activity, including doors opening and closing, among others. With all the reports and the evidence gathered by myself and other paranormal investigators, I think I can safely label this grand old hotel as one of Florida's most colorful Historic Haunts.

THE PIRATE AND THE TURTLE FISHERMAN
John's Pass, Madeira Beach

John's Pass | Photo: Author

The Pirate's Lost Treasure

Steal, pillage and plunder! That was the call to arms of pirates and privateers like John Levique. His story and that of John's Pass became legendary to the world at large, a legend that goes a little something like this. John Levique was a French peasant employed as a cabin boy on a Spanish ship in the 1830's. The ship was taken by pirates, and young John was given the option of joining the pirate crew, or death. Not wanting to die, John decided to become a pirate. Levique ended up becoming Captain of the ship over time, but he wasn't the typical pirate. John refused to kill anyone unjustly and the word spread. Unfortunately, a passive pirate tends to be limited in the amount of treasure he and his crew can collect. This is especially true when idle death threats to captives don't yield confessions of hidden treasures

With an understandably short pirate career over, Levique walked away with only one small chest of gold. He buried it on the west coast of Florida, where he retired, and took on a new persona as a turtle farmer. In 1848, Levique and his partner, a Spaniard named Joseph Silva, decided they would take a shipment of turtles to New Orleans. On their way back from New Orleans they ran into a terrible storm that was wreaking havoc on the coastline. They braved the storm and returned home only to discover the shorelines were completely different. The island where the treasure was buried was cut entirely into two. Gale force winds and high tides had totally changed the way the land was arranged, and it just happened to be centered in the area where the treasure was buried. They ended up sailing their boat in between the two "new" islands into Boca Ciega Bay which is now known as John's Pass. John died in 1873 and his treasure was never found.

In 1976, Captain Wilson Hubbard moved his fishing business here to John's Pass. In 1979 he opened the Friendly Fisherman Restaurant. The boardwalk officially opened in 1980, giving the entire area the appearance of a quaint little fishing village. The area has become a little more commercial since then, but still has a popular appeal. Besides the frequent visitors drawn here to spot the occasional dolphin or by the lure of a great seafood meal, John's Pass boasts frequent visitors of a more paranormal nature.

82

The Ghosts of John's Pass

The most commonly reported ghost is believed by many to be that of John Levique still looking for his treasure. According to the reports and descriptions, a man is often seen walking around in late 1800's garb. The man seems to be searching the area and scoping out the lay of the land. Another possibly related story, features a ghostly boat, seen trying to leave the pass which just seems to vanish into thin air.

There is also another ghost story that centers around two farmers who were Pro-Union during the Civil War. They were murdered by rebel militiamen, and supposedly buried on the south end of the mouth of the pass. People have reported seeing two men in mid 1800's clothes along the area where the bridge is today. In most of these reports they appear to be trying to hide from someone and they are only seen during a new moon.

The last time I was at John's Pass it was a bright and sunny winter day. The weather was just perfect. As I walked under the bridge of John's Pass, I discovered an unusual misty spot. I did a double take trying to figure out what it was. It didn't fit the normal descriptions of an apparition, but it was somewhat humanoid in form and size. It moved slightly towards the water, lingered a moment, then was gone. Other visitors have shared this experience.

Whether the tale of John's Pass is legend or fact, it is still a fascinating story and a fabulous place to visit. With so many places popping up on the boardwalk, maybe the confused ghosts are just trying to figure out what the heck a Hooter's and a Bubba Gump's Shrimp are?

The Bridge under John's Pass where I encountered the mist   Photo: Author

THE 13TH FLOOR
Biltmore Hotel, Coral Gables
....

A Coral Gables Gem

Sometimes it's hard to find a good hotel room. For some people that's reason
enough to build one. In 1924, land owner George Merrick joined forces with John
McEntee Boman, the Biltmore Hotel Magnate. They enlisted renowned architects
Leonard Schultze and S. Fullerton Weaver, famed designers of several buildings,
including New York City's Grand Central Station. Construction began and on January
14th, 1926, the Biltmore Hotel debuted with an inaugural ceremony that was the
social event of the year.

Between 1926 and 1942, the hotel was the most fashionable resort in the country.
Guests were treated to fashion shows held here, along with fantastic galas and balls,
and amazing aquatic shows in the 23,000 square foot swimming pool. The Biltmore
earned such a reputation that during this time some of the most famous names of
Hollywood stayed here. Judy Garland, the Duke and Duchess of Windsor, Ginger
Rogers, Bing Crosby, and even Al Capone, were all guests of this grand hotel.

The Biltmore's time was brief; during World War II the War Department converted
the Biltmore into a huge hospital in 1942, dubbed the Army Air Force Regional
Hospital. It was later renamed the Veteran's Administration Hospital, and continued
serving the public in this capacity until 1968.

When the military took possession of the building, they made many changes in their
efforts to convert the hospital and meet government protocols. Doors were bricked up,
and the beautiful travertine floors were covered in concrete. The building had been
changed from a glamorous hotel into a sterile hospital. After the closing of the
Veteran's hospital in 1968, the building remained vacant from 1973 to 1983. In 1983,
the City of Coral Gables was granted ownership of the old hotel, but the building had
continued to deteriorate since it had been vacated. So, the city initiated a full restoration project to re-invigorate this grand old resort. Four years and fifty-five million dollars later, the Biltmore reopened on New Year's Eve 1987. Her rebirth was short
lived, however, as the hotel closed down in 1990 due to the economic down turn.

Then in July 1992, fans of the hotel had new reason to hope. New owners, led by
Seaway Hotels Corporation, took charge and started another restoration project. This
new renovation would cost forty million dollars and would take ten years to complete.
The result of their efforts was the Biltmore hotel, returned to all her world class excel-
lence. The Biltmore Hotel is still serving the community of Coral Gables and visitors
can see her in all her glory, a beautifully restored hotel full of history and (as I discovered) a few haunts.

Encounters on the 13th Floor

My interest in the stories of paranormal activity in this hotel began with one of my
cousins. He shared a story with me from the summer he spent there as a bell hop. He
and several other bell hops hated going to the 13th floor. He wasn't scared by the
unlucky number of the floor, but by everything that seems to go on there. Almost

84

every time he would take a guests' luggage to the 13th floor, he would experience something. In most cases, when he set the guests bags in their room and then went back out into the hall, the luggage cart would be all the way at the other end of the hallway. In every instance there were no other guests or bell hops to explain the cart's sudden movement. This wasn't his only paranormal experience with the luggage carts. Many times he would be sent to get the luggage of departing guests. He would load the luggage onto a cart, turning briefly to do something or grab more bags. When he turned back around, all the bags would be sitting on the floor next to the cart.

Besides housing guests, the 13th floor was used extensively to treat the soldiers during World War II. Other eyewitnesses have reported seeing full body apparitions of soldiers walking down the hall ways. People have also reported seeing balls of light or other light anomalies floating through the air. In addition, voices have also been reportedly heard at times carrying on full blown conversations in the empty rooms and the halls of the apparently very haunted, 13th floor.

Construction workers during both periods of renovations provided accounts of getting spooked while doing their work. The elevator, for example, would behave erratically, almost always stopping at the 13th or renowned "Bridal Floor".

Supposedly it still continues to do so to this day. These workers also indicated that battery operated tools that were fully charged, quickly lost their charge within minutes of being used on the 13th floor. Many have theorized that the spirits here at the hotel, were using the energy from the power tool's battery packs to materialize themselves.

postcard of the former Biltmore Hotel   Author's Collection

Others reports at the hotel involve hearing voices and being touched by unseen cold hands. Many people described a sensation like someone was there that they couldn't see. Further, the sounds of doors being opened and closed when no one was around have frequently been reported coming from numerous places throughout the hotel.

The Biltmore Hotel is definitely an experience and well worth a visit whether you experience anything paranormal here or not. The 23,000 square foot swimming pool is absolutely amazing, and the other details that make it resemble its original 1924 incarnation are something to see as well. The Biltmore is certainly one of the Miami area's most beautiful "Historic Haunts". If you do manage to visit, be weary of the 13th floor.

POOLSIDE PARANORMAL
The Betsy Hotel, Miami

A Miami Beach Icon

Is there another experience quite like a beach-front stay in Miami? Guests of the consistently highly rated Betsy Hotel would tell you certainly not. The Betsy Hotel is a building created in the traditional colonial style of architecture and designed by L. Murray Dixon. By definition, she is unique among her Art Deco, South Beach neighbors. Construction began on this Miami Beach landmark in 1940, and was completed in 1942. During the first year or so of the hotel's existence, U.S. troops were stationed here during World War II. The hotel now stands as the lone surviving example of Florida/Georgia architecture on Ocean

The Betsy   Photo: Author

Drive. The interior displays beautiful colonial qualities that, thanks to renovations in 2003, and 2009, have been completely restored to their original grandeur.

The Lady By the Pool

A former front desk employee told me that the paranormal activity that occurs here doesn't happen in the building's exquisite lobby bar, or sweeping expansive rooftop, but near its secluded garden pool. A woman wearing a 1940's era long white dress has been seen from time to time walking around the pool area, but always very late at night when most guests have already retired for the evening. She appears to be in deep thought, or deep sorrow. Her mind apparently is elsewhere. She doesn't seem to notice anyone around her. That is, until, someone tries to approach her. Then she vanishes before their eyes.

The former front desk employee who had shared this story with me revealed more details behind the female apparition. These details were verified by an older gentleman, who also worked there for many years. He claims that the woman came here in the 1940's to surprise her husband. The man was one of many stationed here. When she found him, she was surprised to see him in the company of another woman. The man became enraged that she showed up unannounced, and the following day his wife was found drowned in the pool. Did he murder her? Did she drown herself when she found out about the affair? Who knows what parts (if any) of the story are real and which are legend? What is known is that many people have reported seeing this mysterious poolside apparition. The woman's tale is a fascinating story, and the hotel is a beautiful place to stay while visiting South Beach. It is rich in history, culture, design and easily qualifies as a Florida "Historic Haunt".

THE IMPACT OF VERSACE
Versace Mansion, Miami Beach

A Place Fit for a King

Why would anyone travel to Miami and not visit its beautiful beaches? Located along this, popular sun-worshippers paradise was the Versace Mansion. When it was originally built in 1930, it was known as the Casa Casuarina and was built by architect, philanthropist, author and political reformer Alden Freeman. After Freeman's death in 1937, the mansion was turned into apartments by Jacques Amsterdam, who renamed it, "The Amsterdam Palace." It was a place that artists flocked to seeking their future in the art world. In 1992, Gianni Versace, another artist and the "king" of Italian fashion design, purchased the mansion and completely restored it. He even put his own touch on it by adding a south wing, a swimming pool, and a garden to the estate.

The Shot Heard Round the World

On July 15th, 1997 televisions everywhere echoed with the unfortunate news that Versace had been shot down on the front steps of the mansion while returning home from his morning walk. Police discovered that Andrew Cunanan was the killer, and had shot Versace in cold blood. A few days later, Andrew Cunanan turned the same gun he used on Versace on himself while out on his boat. To this day, no one knows the real reasons why Cunanan shot Gianni Versace before turning the gun on himself. No letter was found, and many parts of the murder remain a mystery

A Haunted Estate

Since the murder, a restless spirit has been encountered by many visitors throughout the building. Phone calls are placed to the police department on a weekly basis. Callers reported hearing gun shots coming from inside the estate. When police arrive and investigate the grounds, nothing is found. While these calls were more frequent directly after the murder (when the place was still vacant and locked up), they persist to this day. Many people feel that the grounds are haunted. Several witnesses have reported paranormal experiences involving Versace. Even more curious is the fact that many people have owned the estate or lived there after the murder. They have all experienced extreme financial problems and mishaps.

My Experience with Versace

When I came to informally investigate the mansion, it was known as The Villa by Barton G. I walked up the steps to the front of the mansion and was overwhelmed by a very heavy presence. So strong was this feeling that I honestly didn't want to get any closer to the building. My research indicated that many other people had reported having the same heavy, uneasy feeling on the front steps. I stood on the front steps, trying to get past the negative feeling and pausing awkwardly to have my photo taken. I mustered up my courage and was about to continue, before I could go any farther though, an elderly gentleman approached me from inside, and informed me I was standing on the exact spot where Mr. Versace had been shot! That revelation sent chills down my spine. I am not the type to get frightened off easily (wouldn't be much of a paranormal investigator if I did), but I was ready to leave by that point.

The uneasiness intensified and I began to feel nauseous. I left quickly. I have a great respect for the dead. Lingering, or making fun of a spot where someone was murdered feels very disrespectful. To me this is especially true if the victim is still haunting there, and the Versace mansion is most definitely still a "Historic Haunt"!

THE ARTIST AND HIS SIDEKICK
Artist House, Key West

A Woman, Her Husband, and His Doll

Have you ever been scared of a doll? Most people would probably say no, but the focal point of this "Historic Haunt" is one man's
unusual sidekick, his doll. The story begins with "Artist House"
which is located at 534 Eaton Street and is now an inn. It was
believed to have been built between 1890 and 1898. This Colonial
Queen Ann style home is one of the most photographed houses in
Key West. It was also the former home of a widely celebrated Key
West painter by the name of Robert Eugene Otto, and his wife
Anne who was a concert jazz pianist. Robert (who was known as
Gene) and his wife were married in 1930 and moved to Key West.
Anne performed frequently at the Rainbow Room at Rockefeller
Center, but the couple finally returned to and settled in Key West.
It was shortly after they were married that Anne learned about little
Robert.

Robert the doll

Photo: Author

The Eerie Story of Little Robert

Little Robert, more commonly known as Robert the Doll, has received a tremendous amount of
attention. There has been so much written about him that it is hard to distinguish between the
many interpretations. His story is one of the most famous in Key West, if not Florida, making him
a fixture of area ghost tours. While most of the more believable tales of paranormal activity seem
to center on his time with Gene as an adult, there are more sinister stories that describe Robert's
activities during Gene's childhood.

The story of Robert the Doll begins in 1904, when Eugene (or Gene) was given the doll by a
reportedly African or Bahamian servant of the family. The doll, which resembles an early 20th
century American Naval Officer, was stuffed with straw, and reportedly had a slight resemblance
to Gene. These details are common in most accounts, but this is also where some of the stories
begin to differ (and Robert begins to take on a more terrifying reputation). According to these legends, the family's servant became displeased with them, and being skilled in black magic and
voodoo, crafted Robert with a curse. The doll was said to have an eerie quality that scared the
family and young Gene. His parents described hearing Gene talking to the doll, and later learning
that the responses they heard came not from Gene (in a different voice as they originally thought),
but from Robert. The Otto family claimed to hear the doll emit a terrifying giggle, before they
reportedly caught it running from room to room in passing glimpses. Gene would frequently
scream aloud in the middle of the night, his parents would run to his room and furniture would be
knocked over. Gene, looking terrified, would only say "Robert did it!" Neighbors too claimed to
see the doll moving from one window to another while the Otto family was out. Guests of the
family even swore they saw Robert's expression change (depending on the conversation in the
room) right before their eyes. Regardless of whether these stories are true or not, as more and
more things happened in Gene's life, his reply was "It was Robert!" There was a unique bond
between the two, and Gene saw to it that Robert had his own room (The Turret Room) his own

furniture, and his own stuffed animal.

Interestingly enough, besides the neighbor's claims, in most of the reports I researched, there were several instances of school children, walking to school, who claimed the doll was looking at them before disappearing and reappearing in another window. These children also claimed that Robert's facial expressions would change, and that they (like many others) heard the sounds of giggling, running, and things being moved, coming from Robert's room in the Artist House.

Gene & Robert

When Gene first presented the doll to Anne and tried to convey how close they were, Anne thought he was joking. She soon learned otherwise, as Gene spent more and more time with the doll. Gene would paint in Robert's room (claiming the light was better), and was often in Robert's company. As more and more unusual things happened in their home, Anne became used to hearing the familiar "It was Robert!" She grew to hate the doll. After Gene died in 1974, Anne remained in the home. A short time after Gene had passed, Anne called some electricians to come over and do some work. The electricians completed the work, but quickly left claiming they experienced paranormal activity involving Robert. Many even claimed they saw Robert run past them out of the corner of their eye. Anne decided to lock the doll away in a cedar chest in the attic.

New owners purchased Artist House in the later 1970's. They had a little girl. She too made claims that Robert moved about the room, making the various versions of the story even more confusing. In addition, she has reported to this day, that the doll was in fact alive and wanted her dead. Robert was donated to a Key West museum after Anne's death. Artist House is now a restored Victorian Mansion and a popular guest house.

Activity in Artist House

Many people still report hearing activity in Robert's room. They claim to hear laughter and tiny footsteps running around. Gene and Anne are also still frequently reported in the house. Gene has been seen in different parts of the house (perhaps looking for Robert). Anne is most frequently reported in common areas, watching over the house and making sure all is well.

Robert & I

Robert now resides in a glass case at the East Martello Museum, and is reportedly still very active. The legends that still surround this historic doll claim that it is very difficult to capture a photo of Robert without his permission. Visitors have claimed frequent camera malfunctions, orbs of light in the middle of the pictures, and in some cases, extreme bad luck following their visits and their attempts to photograph Robert without his permission. When I visited the museum in 2004, I asked Robert if I could take his picture. I captured many photos of Robert and after reviewing, they later seemed to notice changes to the expression on his face. I noticed something else while at the museum. Robert was facing one way when I first came in and after I made a complete lap around the museum (and came back to tell him goodbye). He was facing a different way. Curious, I asked the woman working the desk if she or anyone else had moved him. She replied, "No ma'am, I am the only one here and I haven't moved from this spot since I opened."

There are still many who claim that Robert is possessed or evil, I disagree. I sensed nothing malicious when I visited Robert. I definitely felt something. Perhaps it's this sense of the unusual that makes Artist House, and its reported paranormal occupants one of Key West's most intriguing "Historic Haunt"!

PAPA'S GHOST
Hemingway Home, Key West

···

The Famous Author and His Cats

It's hardly a visit to the Florida Keys without seeing the infamous Hemingway home. Construction on this Key West icon was started in 1849, and finished in 1851, by Asa Tift. He was a marine architect and salvage wrecker. Tift knew about the weather sometimes encountered in the Keys, so he instituted some brilliant ideas in the construction. He excavated the limestone from the site to build parts of the house, and he built it 16 feet above sea level which makes it the second highest point on the island.

Asa moved here with his wife Anna and their daughter Annie. Mr. and Mrs. Tift had two sons that were born in the home in 1852, and 1854. Unfortunately, a short time later in 1854 (shortly after the birth of their second son) his wife and both their sons died from a yellow fever epidemic that wreaked havoc on the island. Tift never remarried and died in 1889.

In 1931, the renowned author Ernest Hemingway acquired the home for $8000, which at that time was a fairly large sum. Hemingway lived here with his wife Pauline and their two sons, Patrick and Gregory. They lived in the home together from 1931 until 1939; when Hemingway left for Cuba after he and Pauline divorced. Pauline stayed here with their sons until her death in 1951. From 1951 until 1961, the house was vacant and fell into disrepair. Hemingway died on July 2nd, 1961 in Idaho. His sons sold the estate shortly after his death. The house is now a museum, and is considered one of the largest single residential properties on the island.

The house is still full of Hemingway's furniture and memorabilia, much of which was bought by Pauline when she was in Paris. Besides the house and furniture, Hemingway has left another legacy at the house, the cats. Approximately 40 to 50 cats live on the property; many of them are descendants of Ernest Hemingway's original cats. Among these cats are several unique ones which are polydactyl, which means they have six toes. All the cats here are named after famous people, just as Hemingway once did.

For Whom the Ghosts Toll

There have been many reports over the years of paranormal activity at Hemingway's old home. Some of these stories identify ghostly felines, cats from the past, said to still be lingering on the grounds. There have been reported apparitions of fury four legged creatures running around the courtyard area and around the fountain that Hemingway had installed especially for the cats. Other feline sightings mentioned the graveyard on the property, where Hemingway buried the cats after they enjoyed long and happy lives. There are more than cats said to haunt the old Hemingway house. Pauline's spirit has been seen and reported by eyewitnesses, making sure everything is in its place. She doesn't seem to interact with anyone, just goes through her day to day chores taking care of the house.

Hemingway's ghost has also been seen here, but his appearances are much different than Pauline's. He seems to interact with people from time to time by actually acknowledging them. A slight smile at people or a gesture from the balcony has been commonly reported in many of the incidents of paranormal activity. Hemingway is most often seen as a full body apparition standing on this balcony. Witnesses at the top of the lighthouse, admiring the aerial view of the home, describe seeing a man matching Hemingway's description, on the balcony looking up towards them. This "man" waves hello then vanishes right before their eyes. In addition to Hemingway's physical "presence", the sounds of typing coming from his studio can often be heard from outside, even when the house is deserted. Many have suggested in his own paranormal way, he's working on another book.

The Hemingway Home is one of the most beautiful homes on the island, rich in history. It is a tribute to one of the most admired authors in American history. It was at one time the focus of his work and his life, and perhaps even more fitting, his afterlife. To me it remains one of Florida's most amazing Historic Haunts.

90

ABOUT THE AUTHOR
Jamie Roush

Jamie was born in St. Petersburg, Florida. After several unusual encounters at historic sites as a child, Jamie developed a passion for history and the paranormal. She began to research and investigate paranormal sites and stories. She established Historic Haunts Investigations in 2004 to display her research and findings, and provide an outlet where others could share their stories.

She continued her studies in Parapsychology under noted authority in the field Loyd Auerbach. She has gone on to be featured on the cable tv show "Most Terrifying Places in America" and has been proudly featured in several newspaper articles. To this day she continues researching the paranormal, counts several note-worthies in the field as peers and friends, and has even been present at the taping of several shows by famous televised ghost hunting groups.

Jamie is happy to be the Manager of GhoSt Augustine Ltd. Co., one of the most popular ghost tour providers in St. Augustine (believed by many to be the oldest and most haunted city in America).